IMAGES
of America

FOREST HILLS

IMAGES
of America

FOREST HILLS

Margery L. Elfin, Paul K. Williams, and
the Forest Hills Neighborhood Alliance

ARCADIA
PUBLISHING

Published by Arcadia Publishing
Charleston, South Carolina

Library of Congress Catalog Card Number: 2006926896

For all general information contact Arcadia Publishing at:
Telephone 843-853-2070
Fax 843-853-0044
E-mail sales@arcadiapublishing.com
For customer service and orders:
Toll-Free 1-888-313-2665

Visit us on the Internet at www.arcadiapublishing.com

CONTENTS

ACKNOWLEDGMENTS

Many thanks go to all the authors and neighbors of Forest Hills who made this book possible and to the many schools and embassies that provided information. Thanks also go to: the American Institute of Architects Library; the Historical Society of Washington, D.C., Kiplinger Research Library; Forest Hills Citizens Association; Carnegie Institution of Washington; Library of Congress Prints and Photographs Division and Local History and Genealogy Room; Martin Luther King Jr. Memorial Library, Art and Washingtoniana Divisions; Hillwood Museum; American Institute of Physics; Library of American Broadcasting; Chevy Chase Land Company; Chevy Chase Historical Society; and the National Archives and Records Administration. Thanks also go to: editor Gregory J. Alexander, Stephanie Brown, Leonard Burka, Carla Cohen, Heather Corey, Jim Embrey, Eleanor Ford, Andrew J. Glass, Mark Greek, Stanley Ira Hallet, Shaun Hardy, National Park Service ranger Ron Harvey, Faye Haskins, Judith Beck Helm, Michael Henry, Max Hirshfeld, Judy Hynson, Shirley and Marshall Jacobs, Norman Kiess, LeRoy O. King, Brian Kraft, Heather Lindsay, Dorothy Lee, Keith Martin (National Institute of Standards and Technology), Barbara Meade, Jerry McCoy, Rev. Tom Omholt, Travis L. Price III, Reena Racki, Beverly Rezneck, Judith H. Robinson, Mary Rodgers, Lee H. Rogers, Sue Ann Sadler, Dale Sorcher, Robert Truax, Perry Wheelock, Joseph E. Wnuk, and Charles Zito.

A detailed, full bibliography of sources used in this book is available in the Washingtoniana Division of the Martin Luther King Jr. Public Library, as space limitations limited its reproduction in this volume. Images are individually credited, with some of the following abbreviations: MLK: Martin Luther King Jr., Memorial Library, Washingtoniana Division; LOC: Library of Congress, Prints and Photographs Division; HSW: Historical Society of Washington, D.C.; FHCA: Forest Hills Citizens Association; and NIST: National Institute of Standards and Technology.

INTRODUCTION

What defines a neighborhood? Geographic boundaries, of course, are the primary way of examining a land area, but within these borders are layers of history that help explain the development and growth of a place. Who were the people who inhabited the physical space? Why did they choose to live there? How did they change the environment? Today the usual explanation for the popularity of a commercial or residential area is "location." Centuries ago, it could easily have been "geography."

By 1890, nearly a century after Washington became the official capital of the United States, the old administrative distinction between the city and Washington County had faded; the city boundaries were extended to make room for the population that had settled nearby. Forest Hills was regarded as the country and few homes were built before the 20th century. There were a handful of cultivated, large land holdings in the area, but mostly, despite its proximity to the nation's capital, what we now call Forest Hills was countryside and deep woods. The homes that were built were often constructed in the style of farmhouses and summer homes.

During the Civil War, when the city was ringed by a series of Union fortifications, Military Road (roughly Grant Road) was used to transport troops and supplies between the encampments. It was one of the few thoroughfares that traversed Forest Hills. Almost 30 years later, in 1890, the building of the streetcar line up Connecticut Avenue north to Chevy Chase Circle and a bit beyond made Forest Hills an attractive location for builders. It was now accessible to employment downtown, though still untouched by commercial development. Soon real-estate companies and builders began to acquire the large properties and divide them for sale.

The year 1890 was also notable for the establishment of Rock Creek Park; it was to become the eastern boundary of Forest Hills. Even today, one can walk on the Soapstone Valley Trail two minutes away from the traffic noise on Connecticut Avenue and experience the quiet of nature. A resident's memoir of growing up just after World War I in a large stone house at 3000 Albemarle Street before the street was paved, recalls that his family kept a few cows and a pony in the land next to his house. (See page 100.)

By 1929, there was enough population in Forest Hills to warrant the founding of the Forest Hills Citizens Association. Ann Kessler, the author of the history of this association on its 75th anniversary in 2004, says that the association was determined to keep the neighborhood "beautiful and unspoiled" (See Chapter Seven). The maintenance of trees and gardens was a high priority. Since its founding, the FHCA has pursued quality of life issues and taken positions on zoning, beautification, and recreation.

Because this pleasant, tree-shaded neighborhood was not created by one developer, houses, for the most part, were built to individual tastes. Forest Hills remains architecturally eclectic with few "cookie-cutter" blocks. The majority of houses were built in the period between the wars. Many of the grand apartment buildings were constructed along Connecticut Avenue in the 1920s in the economic boom period before the crash. Despite the impact of the Depression, many substantial homes were built in the later 1930s. There was still some vacant land in the 1950s and 1960s, when many split-level homes were constructed to accommodate the need for postwar housing. Building continued throughout the rest of the century, as some lots were sold off, and existing homes were torn down for new construction. Thus Forest Hills does not present a homogeneous architectural "look," which fact makes it an interesting neighborhood in which to walk. Every style of architecture is represented, along with all varieties of landscaping. (See chapter on Domestic Architecture).

There were a number of elegant homes constructed in the affluent 1920s; some of these were the homes of senators, architects, and wealthy entrepreneurs who wanted a presence in the nation's capital. These luxurious homes were later sold to foreign countries to serve as ambassadorial residences: Peru, Malaysia, and Italy are examples. Much later, in the 1970s and 1980s, the international complex was built as a location for nearly 20 embassies. These buildings occupy the former site of the National Bureau of Standards. The University of the District of Columbia is a close neighbor, situated immediately next to the Metro stop.

The Geophysical Laboratory of the Carnegie Institution of Washington overlooked the eastern side of Forest Hills from a high point near Rock Creek Park at Upton Street. Next to it was a small Catholic women's college, Dumbarton. Today the residence of the Dutch ambassador, the Levine School of Music, and the Howard University Law School all enjoy the view. In the valley below to the south is Hillwood, the former home of Marjorie Merriweather Post.

The story of Forest Hills is a story of change in population and in the use of physical space, as in any vital urban area. Yet throughout the neighborhood, there are constant reminders of the past, in the rural nature of many alleys and roads, in the huge, old trees, and in the historic, landmark Owl's Nest house. When the Owl's Nest was threatened with destruction, a group of neighbors headed by Gary Stevens founded the Forest Hills Neighborhood Alliance to save it. In the course of that effort, a team of volunteers organized a History Day and began to explore other aspects of Forest Hills's past. It was the strong turnout on that day that generated enthusiasm for our neighborhood's history and inspired many residents to support the writing of this book.

FOREST HILLS TIMELINE

1608	American Indian tribes living in Rock Creek are described by John Smith in his journal. A quarry called Rose Hill at Albemarle Street and Connecticut Avenue held the largest deposit of steatite (known as soapstone) in the vicinity.
1687	By this time, the valley and stream became known as Rock Creek.
18th century	Throughout this century, English kings award land grants in the Washington area, including Forest Hills.
1800	When the government moves from Philadelphia to Washington, the plan for the federal city designed by Pierre L'Enfant does not include Georgetown or land north of Boundary Street (Florida Avenue).
1829	Peirce Mill is constructed.
1887	Sen. Francis Newlands and partners secretly begin to buy up more than 1,700 acres of land along a projected extension of Connecticut Avenue from above Florida Avenue to past the District line in today's Chevy Chase, Maryland.
1890	By this time, the Forest Hills neighborhood has become an official part of the city of Washington.
1890–1892	The trolley line and Connecticut Avenue are built.
1901–1942	The National Bureau of Standards gradually acquires more than 60 acres of land between Tilden and Yuma Streets and Reno Road and Connecticut Avenue for its research facility.
1920s	The boom in apartment house construction extends up Connecticut Avenue to Forest Hills.
1927	Firenze House (what is currently the Italian embassy residence) is built at 2800 Albemarle Street.
1929	Forest Hills Citizens Association is founded.
1930	Murch School opens.
1938	Chevy Chase Ice Palace opens with stores as well as ice-skating, bowling, billiards, and table tennis.
1945	Harry S Truman, living at 4701 Connecticut Avenue, becomes president upon Roosevelt's death in April.
1967	Van Ness Centre commercial building opens.
1980	Van Ness/UDC Metro station officially opens December 5 (although it was operated earlier).
2000	Forest Hills Neighborhood Alliance is founded.

One

EARLY HISTORY
BY MEL ELFIN

In 1588, when Spanish explorers first visited the Potomac region, the area that is now Forest Hills was inhabited by a powerful tribe known as the Piscataways. They were hunter-gatherers who settled near streams like Soapstone Creek, where they fashioned cooking implements and arrowheads in an area later known as the Rose Hill quarries. Located at the intersection of what is now Albemarle Street and Connecticut Avenue, the hills, which rose 80 feet above the creek, were leveled in the late 19th century to make way for the trolley line then being built to Chevy Chase. Interestingly the waste materials produced during that excavation are still with us, used as fill for the site of Van Ness Square, which once housed a popular ice-skating rink and is presently the home of Office Depot, Pier One, and Chevy Chase Bank.

The next key date in the history of Forest Hills is 1794, after the War for Independence, when Isaac Peirce bought 2,000 acres of land along both banks of Broad Branch Creek at the outskirts of what was to become the city of Washington. The purchase marked one of the important moments in the very early development of Forest Hills from a sparsely populated collection of farms and woodlands into today's thriving community.

Peirce, an enterprising farmer businessman, gradually transformed his new property into a veritable plantation. Using granite from his own quarries on the creek, he and some of his eight children built several barns, a springhouse, a sawmill, a coach house, and a small distillery. Then, in the 1820s, Peirce, a skilled millwright, tore down an existing gristmill on the west bank of Rock Creek and in its place put up a new mill, which, along with the coach house and springhouse, still stand today.

In July 1861, after the humiliating defeat of Northern forces at the First Battle of Bull Run, the federal government began to realize that the war with the Confederacy was not going to be a brief encounter. Indeed the location of the national capital just across the Potomac from one of the most important and militarily strongest of the Southern states troubled Lincoln and his commanders. The government ordered that a ring of forts and supporting artillery positions be built around Washington, and construction soon began on 26 forts and almost as many supporting artillery batteries on the northern approaches to the city. Fort Pennsylvania (later renamed after Maj. Gen. Jesse Reno) was established atop the highest hill overlooking what is now the intersection of Wisconsin Avenue and River Road, while Fort Stevens was built to block incursions down Seventh Street east of Rock Creek.

Smaller defenses were built between these two heavily fortified positions. Battery Terrill was constructed on the grounds of today's Peruvian Embassy at Thirtieth Place and Garrison Street, and Battery Rossell was built on high ground at the southeast corner of what is now Connecticut Avenue and Fessenden Street. In July 1864, Union troops manning the defenses at both Forts Reno and Stevens proved their importance when they quashed the attempt of Confederate general Jubal Early to raid and capture Washington by attacking not across the Potomac but through the "back door" of Montgomery County. However there is no record that the artillery positioned in Forest Hills ever fired shots in anger.

In effect, the most important role of Forest Hills during the Civil War was to keep open the lines of communications between Forts Reno and Stevens. Not long before the war began, the first primitive east-west route was built from Tennallytown to Brightwood on the other side of Broad Branch Creek, which horses, wagons, and pedestrians crossed at a busy ford. After the war began, this so-called New-Cut Road (eventually renamed in honor of Ulysses S. Grant) became part of the military corridor linking all the fortifications around Washington. Today only a small strip of Grant Road remains in Forest Hills—the portion that runs between Thirtieth and Thirty-Second Streets. West of Thirty-Second Street, Grant Road becomes an alley that dead-ends in the back of the apartments at 4701 Connecticut Avenue.

In *Mr. Lincoln's Forts*, B. F. Cooling notes that the 15th New Jersey Infantry was one of the units detailed to build the forts in late 1862. He quotes Alanson A. Haines, who later recalled the hard work involved in cutting trees and building forts, roads, and rifle-pits. "Long and wearisome seemed these days," Haines said, even though "we enjoy luxuries of which we were soon to be altogether deprived" when sent to the front.

After the War, Washington expanded beyond its old boundary at Florida Avenue, and agriculture became less and less important in the outlying villages. Peirce Mill became a symbol of this transformation when, in 1892, the federal government established Rock Creek Park and acquired the mill. From 1904 until 1934, the building was occasionally leased to individuals for private parties and for use as a teahouse. In 1993, its wooden waterwheel and other mechanical components were judged unsafe and it ceased to function as a mill. However the building remains open as a museum and a National Park Service ranger station. A private organization called the Friends of Peirce Mill are active in raising funds to have the mill function once again as a working museum. Peirce Mill stands as the oldest structure in Forest Hills and one of the oldest in Washington.

Arrowheads frequently found in Soapstone Valley are thought to be the "remains of a tribal enterprise," probably used by the Piscataway tribe for hunting and cooking. William Henry Holmes (1846–1933), seen here, was one of several prominent archaeologists who studied the Soapstone Valley artifacts in the early part of the 20th century. (Holmes *15th Annual Report for the Bureau of Ethnology*, 1893–1894.)

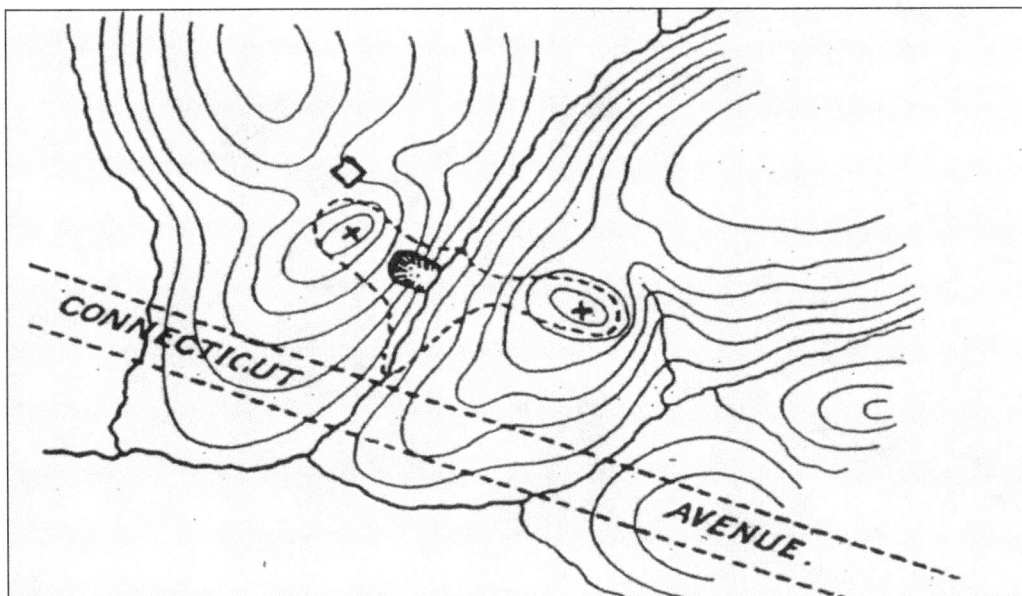

This map by William H. Holmes shows the location of Soapstone Valley, with the area of soapstone outcrop enclosed by the dotted line. The tops of the two hills are marked by crosses. The quarries seem to have first been studied by Elmer R. Reynolds, who in 1878 published a careful description of the site and items he collected. (Holmes *15th Annual Report for the Bureau of Ethnology*, 1893–1894.)

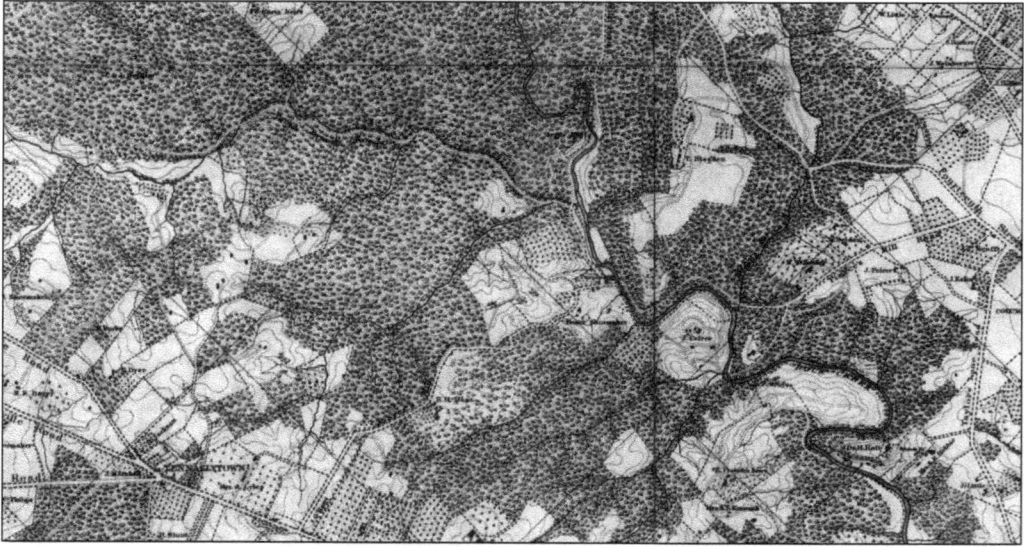

In this detail of the A. *Boschke Map* (drawn 1856–1859), several of the early landowners' homes and buildings can be seen among the heavily treed forest, along with several large tributaries leading to Rock Creek. (LOC.)

Peirce Mill, the earliest business enterprise in Forest Hills, was built on a 250-acre parcel of land purchased by Isaac Peirce in 1794. The mill itself was apparently built in 1829, a date inscribed in the side of the building. During its use as an elegant tearoom in the 1930s, the mill and the adjoining stream were restored by the National Park Service (NPS) in 1934. (MLK.)

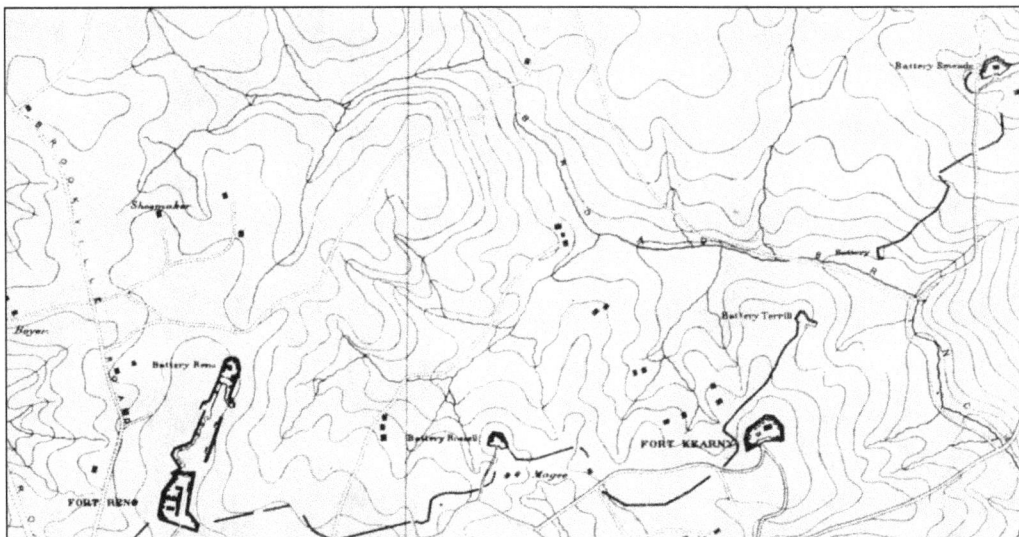

The circle of forts and other defenses built around Washington during the Civil War ran through Forest Hills. This map from General Barnard's *Defenses of Washington* shows the line of rifle pits and field gun batteries that ran eastward from the high point at Fort Reno in Tennallytown to Forts DeRussey and Stevens and beyond. Battery Rossell was located approximately where the Methodist Home stands today. Fort Kearny stood on high ground on today's Thirtieth Place, above Battery Terrill. Old Grant Road (Davenport Street today) can be seen at the bottom, running left to right. (Ron Harvey, NPS.)

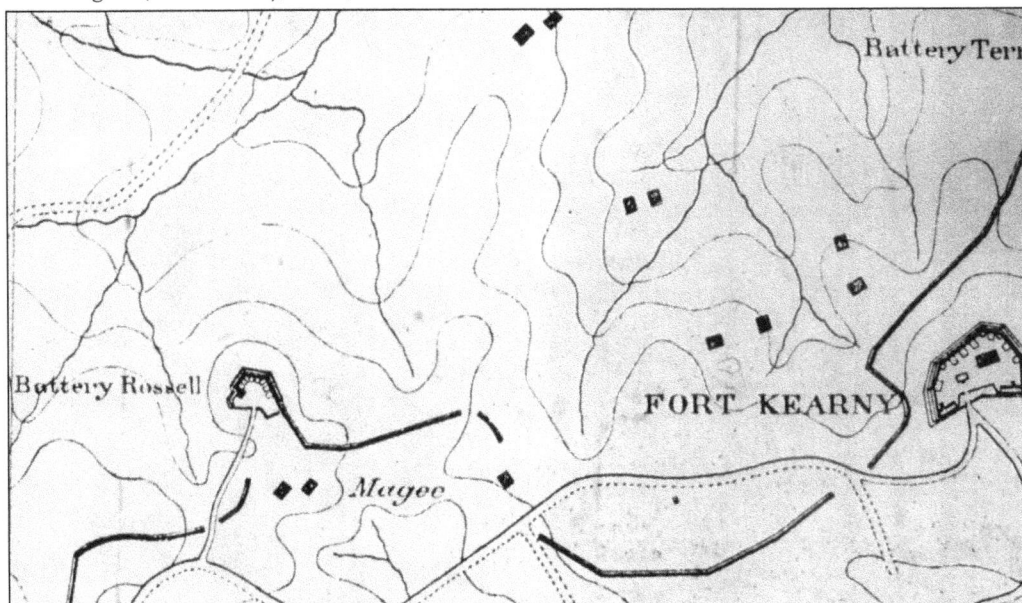

Union soldiers in Forest Hills did not have to come to the aid of the nation's capital during the Civil War, but there was a famous battle close by at Fort Stevens. Toward the end of the war, soldiers camped in Soapstone Valley just before the grand review victory parade down Pennsylvania Avenue in June 1865. This close up of General Barnard's *Defenses of Washington Map* shows Fort Kearny as a rather substantial defense in relation to Battery Terrill. (Ron Harvey, NPS.)

The Garrison Street address of the Embassy of Peru is a reference to the presence of a Civil War battery on the embassy grounds. During Jubal Early's raid in July 1864, detachments of the 151st and 163rd Ohio National Guard were garrisoned at several of these batteries. (Photograph by Mel Elfin.)

Grant Road exists today in Forest Hills in only a small section between Thirtieth and Thirty-Second Streets. Other sections of what was once a corridor linking the Civil War military installations have long since disappeared. (Photograph by Mel Elfin.)

Fort Kearny was named for Maj. Gen. Philip Kearny, who was killed in September 1862 during action following the Second Battle of Bull Run. A hot-tempered, controversial leader, he had lost his left arm in the Mexican War. Fort Kearny is described in *Mr. Lincoln's Forts* as having a 320-yard perimeter, "a large lunette with stockaded gorge . . . and it mounted 10 guns with one vacant platform, including one 8-inch siege howitzer (*en embrasure*), three 32-pdr. seacoast guns (*en barette*), three 24-pdr. siege guns (*en embrasure*), and three 4.5-inch rifles (*en embrasure*)." (LOC.)

Winston Churchill was known to be an occasional guest in this house, located at 2600 Tilden Street across from the Peirce Mill barn. The house was known as Cloverdale, and its origins date to 1794, when Isaac Peirce built it for his family. His grandson, Peirce Shoemaker, rebuilt it in 1874. After a period of operating as a whiskey distillery, the house passed out of the Peirce family in 1928; it was purchased by Enos S. Newman, a real-estate agent who lived there with his wife, Grace. Churchill visited later owner Sherman Adams, a powerful White House aide during the Eisenhower administrations. (Photograph by Paul K. Williams.)

Maj. George A. Armes, a retired army officer and Civil War veteran, was one of Senator Newlands's agents in acquiring land in 1890. He later claimed that he had the original idea to extend Connecticut Avenue and that he convinced Newlands and his partners to join him, but Chevy Chase Land Company documents show only that he was hired for several months in 1890 to buy parcels of land along the route. Major Armes lived near Grant Road, next to the route of the new avenue, and was notorious in the Tennallytown area for galloping on horseback across open land and along the roads, sometimes shooting pistols in the air. (Edith Claude Jarvis.)

The Children's Country Home was once one of Forest Hills' best known institutions, founded in 1883 as a place where poor children could enjoy a respite from the heat of downtown Washington in the country air. The first structure was built in the early 1890s, and by 1895, permission to build an extension for use as a hospital was granted. The site for the home was provided thanks to the generosity of Charles C. Glover. According to the *Washington Post*, he gave a beautiful piece of land along Broad Branch Road and bordering Rock Creek Park to the charity. The home could accommodate 40 children who spent a week or two there during the summer months. Occasionally mothers would accompany the youngest. As many as 400 children were served from June to September. These children would have the benefit of "good food, pure air, the free communion with nature, and its curriculum is the simple one of neat and cleanly habits, wholesome system, and the ways of innocence and happiness." The home became one of the most popular charities for debutantes, and many balls were held to raise funds for the children. It was a major feature of Washington social life. Because the board of the home felt the needs of impoverished children in the District were changing,

they wanted a more modern facility. The property was put up for sale, and the home acquired a tract of land in Northeast Washington, where they planned to construct a convalescent hospital for children. By then, the home was such an important Washington institution that Lou Hoover, Pres. Herbert Hoover's wife, laid the cornerstone for the building in November 1929. In 1931, the seven-acre site of the Children's Country Home had been purchased by Ernest H. Daniel, the president of the Carry Ice Cream Company, for his private residence. Daniel died in 1944, but his wife, who was a respected civic leader and philanthropist, lived on in the house until 1957.

Two

CONNECTICUT AVENUE
BY ANNE ROLLINS

Connecticut Avenue north of Calvert Street was built by a private company, which then gave title to the road to Washington, D.C. In order to create a suburban housing development just over the Maryland line, Sen. Francis Newlands (Democrat) of Nevada and his Chevy Chase Land Company literally paved the way and also laid tracks for an electric streetcar line along the new road. Between 1890 and 1892, the company built two substantial bridges, excavated, leveled, and paved five miles of road, and laid streetcar tracks for the entire length.

In the decades after the Civil War, Washington had been gradually expanding northward beyond the old Boundary Street (now Florida Avenue), aided by the convenience of new streetcar service to downtown. Projecting a northwestward extension of Connecticut Avenue from its end at Boundary Street, Senator Newlands by 1887 had selected the site for Chevy Chase just over the Maryland line, close to the city but set at a higher elevation to benefit from cooler breezes in summer. Keeping his plans secret, Newlands, with a few partners and agents, began buying up land along the proposed route. At the same time, he was encouraged by a debate in Congress to set aside a large amount of land for an urban park in the valley of Rock Creek, roughly parallel to the road he envisioned. Local support for the parkland was strong, and a bill establishing the National Zoological Park passed in 1889, followed the next year by legislation creating Rock Creek Park.

By 1890, Newlands and his partners had purchased a patchwork of 1,713 acres stretching from the site of today's Taft Bridge to Jones Bridge Road. When the press learned in the spring of 1890 that a "syndicate" was buying the land for development, Newlands went public and formed the Chevy Chase Land Company. Needing a Congressional charter to build a streetcar line, the partners also bought the Rock Creek Railway Company, which had a charter to construct streetcar service as far as Woodley Park. The charter's terms were changed to allow for extending the streetcar line to the Maryland suburbs, and construction began.

The hilly, stream-cut terrain proved to be more of a challenge than Newlands and his partners had realized when buying the land, and an enormous amount of earth had to be moved during construction. An August 1, 1891, *Washington Star* article noted that "owing to the broken and rugged character of the country, immense fills and cuts were made, some of them as much as fifty feet in depth." In his memoirs, former Chevy Chase Land Company president Edward Hillyer wrote about the area around Soapstone Creek: "The hills had to be cut down by pick and shovel and the valleys filled by horse drawn carts. A good illustration of this operation was the cutting down of what was known as Soapstone Hill on the west side of Connecticut Avenue at Albemarle Street and the earth had to be taken across the Avenue and filled in where the Ice Palace Shopping Center is today [now Van Ness Square], a fill or depth of some forty or fifty feet. In some places a train of small dumping cars with a donkey engine carried the dirt on very narrow gauged rails."

The new road and streetcar service opened up a huge area of Northwest Washington to development, and individuals and organizations, as well as developers, began to build along Connecticut Avenue. In 1901, the National Bureau of Standards bought the first of the many acres it would acquire west of the avenue, along Peirce Mill Road (approximately Van Ness Street today), for its headquarters. Two years later, the presence of the National Bureau of Standards influenced the decision of the Carnegie Institution of Washington to build its geophysical laboratory on land nearby, east of Connecticut Avenue. In 1902, Fernwood Heights, the first residential subdivision along upper Connecticut Avenue, was registered with the District Surveyor's Office.

In this detail of an 1891 G. M. Hopkins real-estate map, Connecticut Avenue Extended is under construction, its path shown by dotted lines. Peirce Mill Road, near the bottom of the map, was built to connect the mill to the Georgetown and Rockville Road (now Wisconsin Avenue), and its winding course followed the dictates of the topography. Farther north, Military Road, parts of which were also called Grant Road, was a remnant of the road that connected the circle of defenses around Washington during the Civil War. Most of Chappell Road east of Connecticut was later renamed Thirty-Sixth Street. The sparsely settled area that is Forest Hills today was a crazy quilt of land holdings, but the Chevy Chase Land Company was a major landowner, especially along Connecticut Avenue. (LOC.)

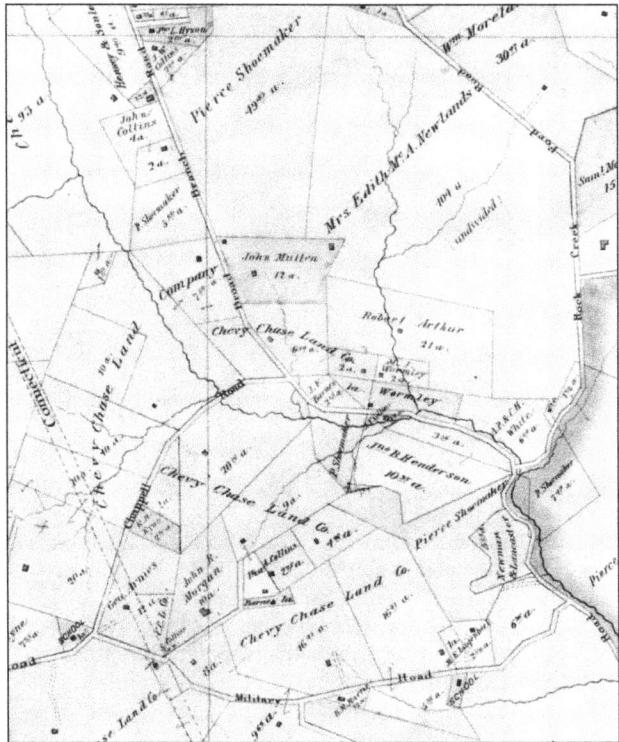

Sen. Francis Newlands of Nevada was convinced that the city's expansion would continue into the rolling, gradually rising land beyond Boundary Street (now Florida Avenue) and the Rock Creek Valley. His plan was to "establish a suburban town, connect it with Washington by a railroad line which will furnish quick transit, and then let the improvement in value at both ends build up in the immediate [i.e., intermediate] property." He sited the development of Chevy Chase just over the District line in Maryland in part so that residents there would have voting rights. (Chevy Chase Land Company.)

An early view south along Connecticut Avenue in Woodley Park shows where the road and streetcar line turned east (left) to cross the iron trestle bridge over Rock Creek Valley, visible in the center left distance. The bridge was built at Calvert Street because the civil engineer hired by Newlands to survey the road's proposed route believed that it would be too costly to grade the hill where the existing Connecticut Avenue ended at Florida Avenue and then cross Rock Creek Valley at the site of today's Taft Bridge. Even after the Taft Bridge was completed in 1907, the streetcar continued to cross at Calvert Street. (Cleveland Park Historical Society.)

Streetcars crossed Rock Creek Bridge at Calvert Street and connected with other streetcar lines to downtown. Built in 1891–1892 by the Edgemore Bridge Company for the Rock Creek Railway, the bridge was 755 feet long and 125 feet high. In 1934, when construction began on its replacement, the present Duke Ellington Bridge, the entire metal bridge was shifted 80 feet downstream on rails pulled by horses and connected to realigned tracks and road surfaces at either end with traffic across the bridge restored in just 48 hours. The old bridge continued to carry traffic until the new bridge was ready the following year. (LOC.)

In the early 19th century, John Adlum owned 230 acres in the area west of Connecticut Avenue and north of Tilden Street. This 1906 photograph shows the remains of his house, which stood near Peirce Mill Road, not far from today's Tilden Street. Naming his estate the Vineyard, the Revolutionary War veteran raised 22 varieties of grapes, including the Catawba, which was used in making wine. The house was demolished in 1911 to make way for an expansion of the National Bureau of Standards. (LOC.)

Fairfield was the home of Civil War veteran Maj. George A. Armes, who was one of Senator Newlands's agents in acquiring land in 1890. Situated on Connecticut Avenue approximately near today's Ellicott Street, the house had been turned into a hotel and boarding house by the 1890s, when this photograph was taken. In August 1906, the *Washington Post* reported Armes's complaint that the city had made a cut of 27 feet in front of his property some years before and now proposed to grade the road another eight feet lower. He also claimed that the grading was being done simply to provide dirt to "fill in Albemarle street between Grant road and Connecticut Avenue." The hotel was not a success, and Major Armes gave up the hotel business and moved from Forest Hills in 1912. (Robert Truax.)

Ethel Armes, a daughter of Maj. George Armes, watched the construction of Connecticut Avenue as it passed close by their house. She was fascinated by a Baltimore and Ohio Railroad locomotive that pulled trains along the new streetcar tracks, hauling loads of building materials and excavated soil. In a *Washington Post* article in October 1892, the 16-year-old told how she befriended the crew members, who, she claimed, let her ride in the cab and even run the locomotive:

Before the electric cars were running on Connecticut Avenue extended, and the tracks were uncompleted, one day we were startled by the loud, shrill blast of a whistle and a terrific noise as an engine came thundering by. A train of trucks, beside the caboose and coal car were all attached. Half an hour later it returned with loaded trucks on its way to the circle . . . A wild whim seized me—what a wonderful thing if I could say I knew how to run an engine—a real Baltimore and Ohio engine.

So one evening two of my numerous brothers accompanied me, and tremblingly we slowly made our way to the hissing, steaming thing. No one was there. Growing bolder as the minutes sped by, we gathered wild flowers from the woods on each side and gayly decorated "the big iron horse." We climbed up in the cab, and . . . suddenly heard footsteps. . . . Expecting a ferocious scolding, I timidly stood before the tall man who had just come up. . . .

"I—I was putting flowers on her," said I nervously. "I hope you don't mind?"

"Not at all," he answered with a slight smile, taking off his hat. . . . He was the fireman.

"I think I will have to go now, but I will try to come tomorrow. May I run it?"

"Certainly, if you should like to try."

Accordingly, the next day I received my first lesson. . . . She wasn't hard to run: the difficult part came in learning the uses of the innumerable pieces of machinery about it, and it was pretty hard to pull the whistle cord right, but I succeeded at last. Almost every day I was on 178. . . . Every cross road had a name of its own, houses were stations, and it was as though 178 was on a miniature main line. . . .

As we came thundering down the grade from Peirce's Mill road, one hand on the throttle and one on the whistle cord, and as we rushed nearer Soapstone Hollow, I would let forth a terrific blast, which echoed its shrill notes for miles around. How I loved to pull the throttle wide open, feel the great, throbbing engine advance forward, propelled by the strong power of the steam, to hear the wild, screaming, discordant voice of the whistle which I always made!

One day my sister and some friends got on the engine [manned only by Ed Shipley, the fireman]. I, greatly to my satisfaction, was elected engineer.

Sometimes, as every one knows, engines get contrary, and that day she certainly was so, almost beyond my control. We were going down Shoemaker's Cut at a pace I warrant you was not slow. . . . We were going at a fearful rate across a dangerous part of the avenue. Shutting the throttle off, I tried to pull the reverse bar back to stop. I couldn't move it. The engine was rocking from side to side, turning one dizzy to look down the fearful depth of the hollows on either side. . . . [Shipley] worked the bar, now nearly beyond his management, back and forth until he had stopped her.

Ethel Armes's flair for writing supported her throughout her life. After working briefly for the *Washington Post*, she became a freelance writer, publishing several books on a variety of subjects. In the late 1920s, Ethel Armes was instrumental in the founding of the Robert E. Lee Memorial Foundation. While employed by the foundation as national secretary, she published *Stratford Hall: The Great House of the Lees* in 1936. She died in 1945 at the MacDowell Colony in New Hampshire.

The original streetcars to Chevy Chase, such as these from 1892–1895, also noted the zoo as a destination, for the new park proved to be very popular with Washingtonians. Passengers to and from the zoo helped sustain the railway in its earliest years, while Chevy Chase and the areas around Connecticut Avenue slowly developed. In "Suburban Washington as a Place of Residence," a promotional booklet produced by the Citizens Northwest Suburban Association in 1901, the streetcar service was extolled: "Few suburbs of cities anywhere possess rapid transit facilities equal to those of this delightful section of the District. It is traversed from southeast to northwest by . . . electric cars upon which one may ride from the heart of the city to the District limits in thirty minutes for a single fare, six tickets being sold for twenty-five cents." (Robert Truax Collection, Chevy Chase Historical Society.)

In the hot summer, open streetcars were cooler and provided a breezy way to travel out to Chevy Chase Lake for a picnic or even for just a pleasant ride through the countryside, with a top speed of 17 miles an hour. (LeRoy O. King Collection, Chevy Chase Historical Society.)

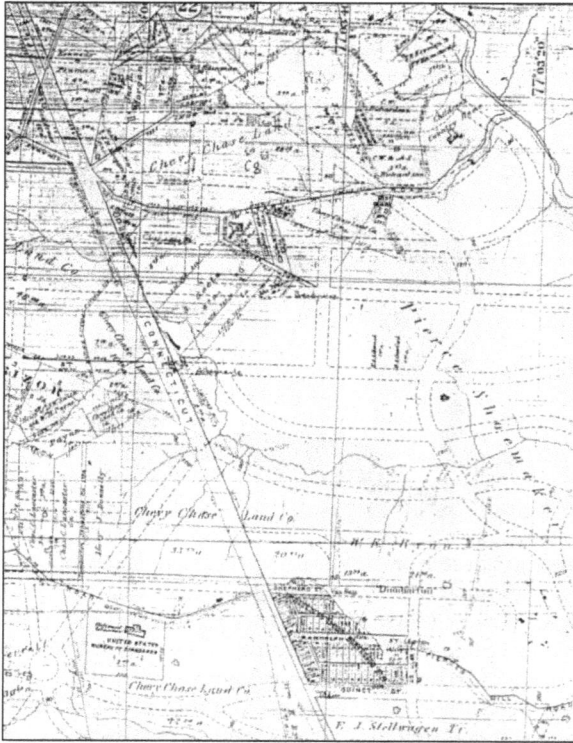

Ten years after the completion of Connecticut Avenue Extended, the future Forest Hills was still very sparsely settled. On this 1903 Baist real-estate map, planned streets are indicated with dotted lines. Most of the early roads were eventually replaced by the city's street grid, but some, such as Gates and Grant Roads (called Military Road here), survive in short, disjointed segments to this day. Quincy Street, running along the southern edge of Fernwood Heights, was renamed Tilden, Randolph became Upton, and Shepherd became Van Ness. To the north, Major Armes's house appears just west of Connecticut Avenue and above Military Road, and the large house shown between Military and Gates Roads, labeled "Wm. Crounse," is Owl's Nest. (LOC.)

In 1919, National Bureau of Standards (NBS) physicist William Meggers flew a small plane over Northwest Washington and took a number of photographs. In this view from above the NBS campus toward the north and east, the intersection of Connecticut Avenue and Albemarle Street is visible toward the upper right, below the open fields and greenhouse of the Springer nurseries. The Springers were florists, and their land was bordered by Gates Road on the northeast, where they located their house. The last of this open land was sold in 1949 to the developers of Albemarle House and Brandywine apartments. (American Institute of Physics.)

In this early-1920s view of Connecticut Avenue at Van Ness Street, looking northwest, an NBS building is visible to the left, and a small store faces out toward the intersection. Development on upper Connecticut Avenue proceeded slowly during the early 20th century, but the First World War brought tremendous growth to Washington, and some of that growth made its way out to Forest Hills and the suburbs beyond. The District's zoning laws in 1920 designated Connecticut Avenue for medium density residential development, with four "business islands" between Woodley Park and the district line. Two of these commercial areas were from Van Ness Street to Albemarle Street and from Davenport Street to Fessenden Street. This was a compromise between the zoning committee's initial idea to designate all of Connecticut Avenue for commercial development and the counter proposal by the Chevy Chase Citizens' Association to maintain it as a residential street, decrying the image of one of the "principal gateways to the National Capital . . . lined with stores." (MLK.)

In 1949, amateur photographer John Wymer took this picture along the east side of Connecticut Avenue between Upton and Van Ness Streets. This block and the block to the south, between Tilden and Upton Streets, were the only blocks along Connecticut Avenue in Forest Hills lined with private row houses. (Wymer Collection, HSW.)

These houses at the northeast corner of Upton Street and Connecticut Avenue were built in 1903–1904 and designed by Leon Emile Dessez for Senator Newlands as owner/developer. By 1907, the Army and Navy Preparatory School had moved into 4101–4105 Connecticut Avenue, and within a few years, it also occupied houses at 4107 and 4109 Connecticut Avenue and 2969 Upton Street (visible on the right side of the photograph). In 1910, the school built Todd Hall, designed by architect A. B. Mullett and Company, at 2955–2961 Upton Street; it is still in use today as part of the Edmund Burke School. By 1948, when John Wymer took this photograph, 4103 Connecticut Avenue, to the left, was being used for a convalescent home. (Wymer Collection, HSW.)

In 1924, the Devitt School bought Todd Hall from the Army and Navy Preparatory School, which relocated outside the city. Devitt students are shown here leaving Todd Hall in the mid-1930s. Founded in 1919 in Georgetown by former Western High School teacher Dr. George R. Devitt, the school moved to Forest Hills in 1924 and thrived there until 1951, when it became part of the Longfellow School in Bethesda. (MLK.)

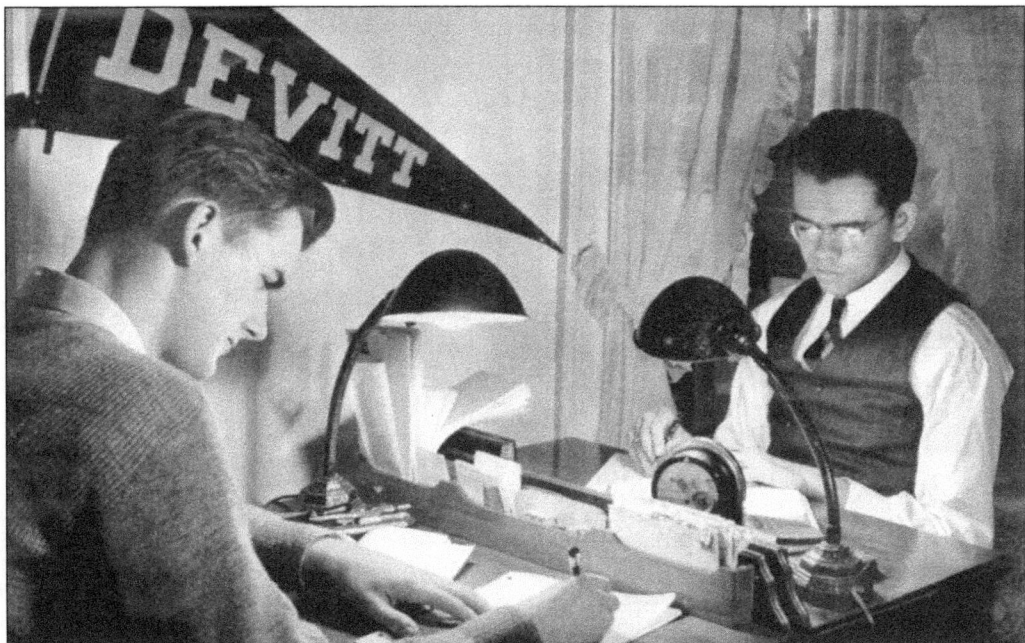

These impeccably tidy students were used to illustrate the 1937 Devitt School brochure. A four-year college preparatory high school for boys, Devitt also provided courses for those who wanted to prepare for the entrance exams for West Point and the Naval Academy, as well as for the Coast Guard and "Air Services." (MLK.)

Some of Devitt's students boarded, and the school leased attached stone houses at 4107 and 4109 Connecticut Avenue for dormitory space. Here a few boarders lounge on the front porch of the building and gaze across a quiet Connecticut Avenue toward the NBS campus, c. 1937. (MLK.)

PONCE de LEON
4514 Connecticut Avenue Northwest

The Ponce de Leon, 4514 Connecticut Avenue, was one of six large apartment houses built along the avenue in Forest Hills between 1927 and 1930, including 4550, the Frontenac; 4700, Parker House; 4701; 4707; and 4800, Davenport Terrace. This building boom and other development brought many residents to the area, and construction along the two commercial strips reflected their needs. By 1930, the stretch between Van Ness and Albemarle Streets was still dominated by three service stations, with a deli, country store, and barbecue restaurant; in the block north of Fessenden were five grocery stores, a drug store, paint store, plumber, tailor, dry cleaner, florist, shoe repairman, the Chevy Chase Woman's Exchange, and two gas stations. (http://www.ancestory.com.)

David L. Stern designed the Ponce de Leon in 1928 in a Spanish Revival style and lived there upon its completion. The use of period motifs suggestive of other eras and sometimes exotic places was popular among architects in the 1920s. The lobby interior is seen at right, and the building has been placed on the National Register of Historic Places. (Photograph copyright Beverly Rezneck.)

In 1927–1928, Harry M. Bralove built three apartment buildings in the 4700 block of Connecticut Avenue: 4707 Connecticut Avenue, shown here; 4701, next door; and the Parker House, across the street. A greatly expanded federal government and postwar inflation produced a housing crunch in Washington, which in turn spurred a boom in apartment construction throughout the city. In 1920, Connecticut Avenue was zoned for apartment house development to a depth of 100 feet from the street. A 1910 law restricted most apartment buildings to five stories, to keep housing density low, but that was changed in 1930 to eight stories. (Wymer Collection, HSW.)

Built in 1927 for the middle class, 4701 Connecticut Avenue still incorporated many of the quality features more typical of older, grander apartments downtown. Architect George T. Santmyers lavished architectural detail in the building's lobby, shown here in 1974, and most of the roomy apartments had entrance foyer, parlor, dining room, kitchen, two bedrooms, bath, and porch. (MLK.)

Harry S Truman and his family lived at 4701 Connecticut Avenue from January 1941 to April 1945, thereby providing the building its enduring nickname, the Truman House. Here Truman, wife Bess, and daughter Margaret pose in their comfortable living room, complete with piano, in 1942. (Office of War Information, Courtesy Harry S Truman Library.)

Davenport Terrace, between Davenport and Ellicott Streets, was built by Harry Wardman and opened in 1929. The four buildings were set on a three-acre lot, with a large open, grassy area bordering on Connecticut Avenue, and are distinguished by the varied and gracious detailing for which Wardman was noted. This 1949 view by John Wymer looks across Connecticut Avenue to the northwest. In the 1970s, the space was considered too valuable to be left vacant, and the Holladay Corporation filled the space with the Ellicott House apartment building. (Wymer Collection, HSW.)

4801 Connecticut Avenue

Apartment construction in Forest Hills halted with the onset of the Depression, but in 1938, Realty Mortgage and Guaranty Company built 4801 Connecticut Avenue at the corner of Davenport Street. Architect David Stern's art moderne design departed from the neoclassical styles of its neighbors (and his designs a decade earlier), and the basement included parking space for 100 cars, a far greater number than earlier apartments and a reflection of the increasing impact of the automobile. (James Goode Collection, HSW.)

The round glass brick entrance lobby of 4801 Connecticut Avenue is echoed by a circular, stainless steel canopy suspended over the semicircular drive in front. The lobby's terrazzo floor is designed in a sunray pattern. (James Goode Collection, HSW.)

31

The last streetcars ran along Connecticut Avenue on September 14, 1935. This advertisement ran that day in the *Washington Star* to acquaint customers with the new buses, routes, and numbering system. (MLK.)

The Methodist Home for the Aged was built between Ellicott and Fessenden Streets in 1926 to replace its aging and outgrown facility at 601 M Street NW. Designed by Arthur B. Heaton, one of the premier architects of the day, the new home originally had 60 bedrooms arranged so that each room got sunlight at some point during the day. There were also the dining room shown, reception and living rooms, chapel, kitchen, infirmary, and rooms for the nurses. The home has built extensive additions over the years to meet changing needs. (Methodist Home.)

Construction of the Methodist Home took just 10 months in 1926. In this April view, Connecticut Avenue is visible beyond the building's foundation, running the width of the image. Development spreading east from the old Tennallytown is evident in the center background. (Methodist Home.)

Engine Company 31 firehouse was built in 1930 between Ellicott and Fessenden Streets, one of four engine houses constructed between the wars with tall hose towers. The tower was used for hanging the hoses after use to dry them out, but this tower proved an ironic liability when it was struck by lightning in July 1938. Little damage was reported, and the tower remained standing for at least another decade. The tower was eventually shortened, probably for greater ease of maintenance, and the original weather vane, representing firemen running toward flames with axes at the ready, was restored and placed again on top of today's shorter tower. (Jack Gerhart Collection.)

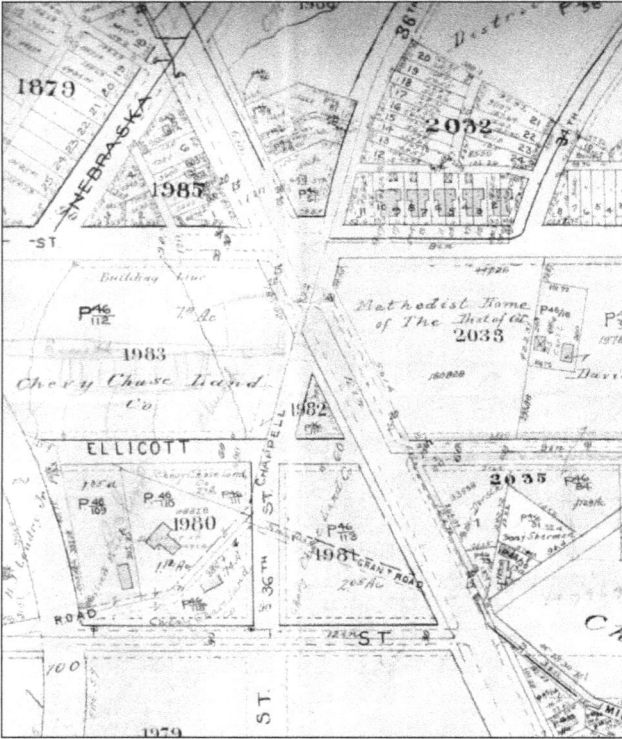

In this detail of a 1925 Baist real-estate map of Connecticut Avenue (running diagonally from the upper left to the bottom center of the map) between Fessenden Street and Nebraska Avenue, Capital Traction Substation Number 4 shares the east side of the avenue with a single gas station. Occasional power substations were necessary to relay the electricity to run the heavier streetcars introduced around 1912, and this brick building served that purpose until 1935, when streetcar service ended along Connecticut Avenue. Capital Traction Company owned the building until 1939, renting it out for use as an automobile showroom, and eventually it was replaced by a larger brick structure that has housed Safeway, Higger's Drugstore, and now CVS. (Paul K. Williams Private Collection.)

Hot Shoppes arrived in Forest Hills in 1930 and quickly became popular, especially with young people. In this image from the early 1930s, the staff is gathered in front of the restaurant at 4340 Connecticut Avenue, just south of Yuma Street. Note the steep hill in the background, cut away to make room for the building and its parking lot. (HSW.)

John Collier, a photographer for the Office of War Information, took these photographs in December 1941 at the Connecticut Avenue Hot Shoppe. Judging by the men's ice skates under the table and the women's skates slung over the backs of their seats, these young people probably had either just come from or were on their way to the Chevy Chase Ice Palace across the street. (LOC.)

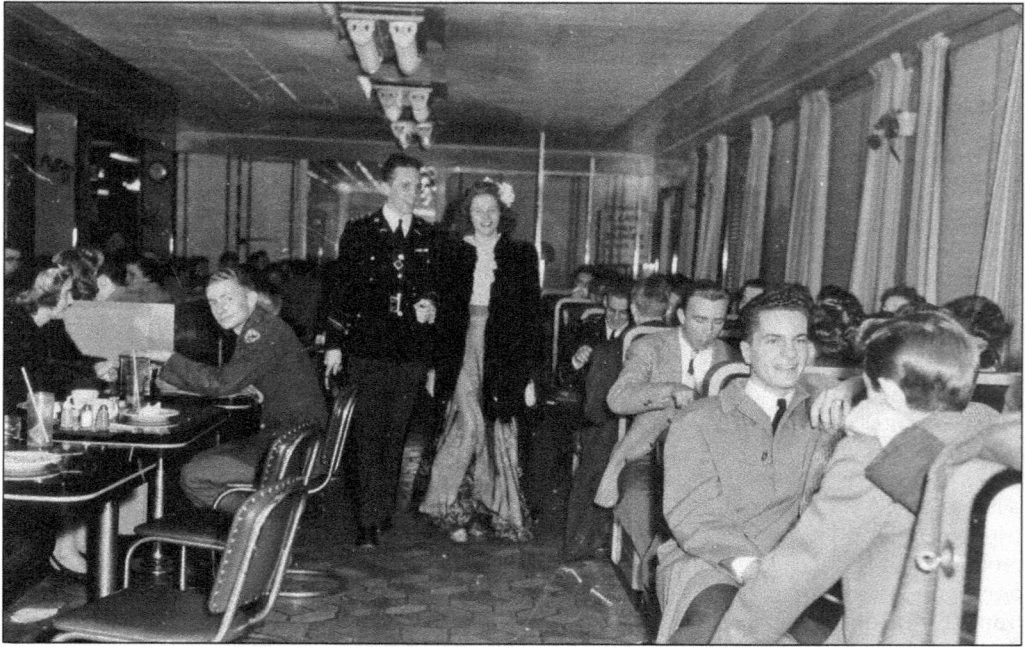

Esther Bubley, another photographer for the Office of War Information, visited the Connecticut Avenue Hot Shoppe in October 1943 and found this group of Wilson High School students gathering after the Regimental Ball. (LOC.)

The Colony House furniture store opened at 4244 Connecticut Avenue in 1937; it was designed by Arthur B. Heaton to resemble the facade of the Raleigh Tavern in Williamsburg, Virginia. The store claimed to showcase "hundreds of authentic recreations of Early American, Colonial and 18th Century pieces." Colony House's first store closed in 1975 to make room for Metro construction. (Jerry A. McCoy Postcard Collection.)

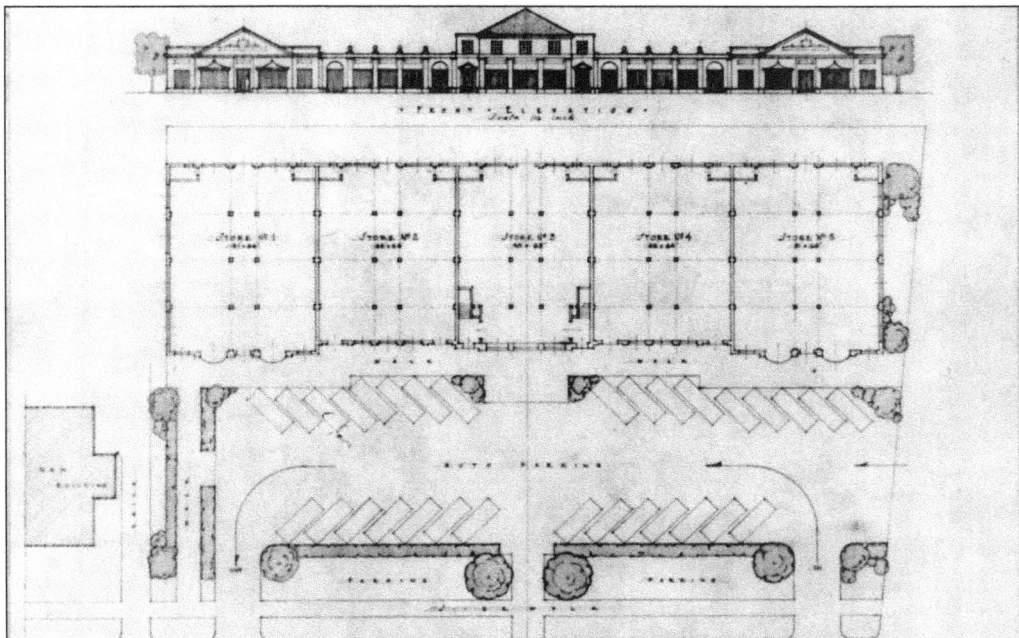

Architect Arthur B. Heaton produced these plans for a "store group" at Connecticut and Idaho (now Windom) Avenues, adjacent to the Colony House furniture store, for the Chevy Chase Land Company in 1937. The company owned many acres of land along Connecticut Avenue and planned from the beginning to develop areas when appropriate. Following on the success of his Park and Shop in Cleveland Park several years before, Heaton designed a similarly classical and small-scale shopping center with parking in front. This center was never built, however. (LOC.)

The elegant Franklin Simon clothing store opened at 4250 Connecticut Avenue in 1948, the year of this photograph by John Wymer. Despite its generally classical exterior, the building's interior was sleekly modern. Herbert B. Beidler of Chicago designed the store for the Chevy Chase Land Company. (Wymer Collection, HSW.)

The Gottscho-Schleisner company was hired to photograph the new Franklin Simon store in October 1948: this view looks toward the front entrance at left and the approach to the fur and clothing departments toward the entrance. (LOC.)

The Chevy Chase Ice Palace opened in November 1938 below the intersection of Connecticut Avenue and Albemarle Street. Taking the concept of the Park and Shop one step further, owner Garfield I. Kass built retail shops on the ground floor, and on the floor above, he added Washington's first indoor ice-skating rink. On floors below street level, he installed table tennis, pool tables, and a bowling alley with 41 lanes. The original stores included Woolworth's, A&P, Peoples Drug Store, and Best and Company, and in 1941 the Washington Daily News called the Palace "probably the swankiest shopping center in town." Despite the huge popularity of the ice-skating and bowling facilities through the 1940s, Kass claimed that the complex would not be financially viable without the store rentals. (Wymer Collection, HSW.)

Office of War Information photographer Edwin Rosskam caught this group of skaters at the ice rink in November 1942. The 50-by-175-foot rink was an instant success, drawing as many as 400 skaters of all ages daily. Some signed up for lessons with the rink's professionals, and a few local schools gave physical education credit for skating. (LOC.)

THE WINTER CLUB OF WASHINGTON, INC.

1941 - 1942 Season

This is to certify that *Sarah Alice Rice*

is a member of The Winter Club of Washington

Chevy Chase Ice Palace

Membership is not transferable

No. *97*   Members skate at their own risk

Ed. F. Snell   *Helen M. Silvy*

President   Treasurer

THIS CARD MUST BE PRESENTED AT THE DOOR.

The popularity of ice-skating gave rise to skating clubs, some purely social and some associated with federal agencies, including the FBI, Federal Reserve, IRS, and Agriculture Department. Each club had designated times when the rink was reserved for its members. During the Second World War, the Washington Figure Skating Club sponsored an annual Christmas party to benefit the war effort. In 1941, the theme was "Smokes for the Yanks," followed the next year by a Christmas War Stamp Party, at which the club sold war stamps as admission tickets, with war bonds as door prizes. (HSW.)

A pair of skaters takes a break in the snack bar at the Chevy Chase Ice Palace, where skates were welcome, in this 1942 photograph by Edwin Rosskam. Shirley Scher Jacobs was a teenager in Forest Hills in the 1940s. She recalls many evenings out at the Hot Shoppes, a popular gathering place for high schoolers across the street from the Ice Palace. Marshall Jacobs, Shirley's husband, remembers their first date, when he took her to play pool at the Ice Palace. (LOC.)

The Chevy Chase Ice Palace also included 41 bowling alleys, where this young woman is demonstrating her style in an April 1942 image by Office of War Information photographer John Ferrell. Bowling had been popular since the 1920s, but the sport boomed during the Depression and again during the war, with leagues and lanes throughout the city and hundreds of teams sponsored by companies large and small. Shortly before the Ice Palace opened, the *Washington Post* noted the need for more lanes, calling Washington the "duckpin bowling center of the United States." Although the official competitive season ran from September to April, the Ice Palace was air conditioned, encouraging the more relaxed summer leagues, which tended to be mixed teams of men and women. During the school year, some Alice Deal Junior High School students bowled there for gym credit. (LOC.)

Table tennis was another popular activity at the Chevy Chase Ice Palace, although photographer John Ferrell did not note whether this scene was during one of the "Special Ladies Nights" advertised on the sign on the wall. (LOC.)

Shown is the interior of Farr's Jewelers, one of the stores that leased space on the ground floor of the former Ice Palace. From the early 1950s to the late 1980s, owners Vance and Dorothy Farr sold and repaired jewelry, watches, and silver to customers who could park for free in front of the store. (Jerry A. McCoy Postcard Collection.)

By 1950, recreational ice-skating rinks were no longer viable economically, and both the Ice Palace and Uline Arena closed their rinks. In August 1950, the rink space at the Ice Palace was leased by the Evening Star Broadcasting Company to house its WMAL-TV operations. The second floor was renovated for three studios, and the station began broadcasts there in October. The next month, Ruth Crane, one of Washington's pioneer female telecasters, began a live television version of her WMAL-AM radio show, *The Modern Woman*. Here Crane faces the camera, prompted by a distinctly low-tech cue card. (Library of American Broadcasting, University of Maryland.)

Jackson Weaver, shown with Ruth Crane on the set for *The Modern Woman* in the old ice-skating rink space, was Crane's cohost on both the radio and television versions of the program. Part of the set was a full kitchen where Crane demonstrated cooking and introduced new products. Broadcast one night a week for the first three years, the show became a daily afternoon program as WMAL-TV increased its broadcast hours beyond the evening. Crane retired in 1955. (Library of American Broadcasting, University of Maryland.)

In this *c.* 1940 aerial view looking down Connecticut Avenue from Albemarle Street, the Chevy Chase Ice Palace and shopping center is in the left foreground, across the street from the Hot Shoppe. Traveling south, one would pass a scattering of stores, car dealers, and gas stations, with the large NBS buildings dominating the west side. Many of the commercial buildings on the east side would be demolished in the 1960s to make way for the Van Ness Centre, and the Van Ness apartment buildings would fill much of the open land between there and Soapstone Valley. (MLK.)

In April 1949, John Wymer photographed scenes along Connecticut Avenue in Forest Hills. Here the Hot Shoppe, partially hidden by a tree, sits between two automobile dealerships. The Ponce de Leon apartment building is visible above Albemarle Street, with the top floors of the Frontenac rising just above it in the distance. (Wymer Collection, HSW.)

Continuing north on Connecticut Avenue in April 1949, John Wymer photographed many of the stores on the east side of the block from Nebraska Avenue, in the foreground, toward Fessenden Street. (Wymer Collection, HSW.)

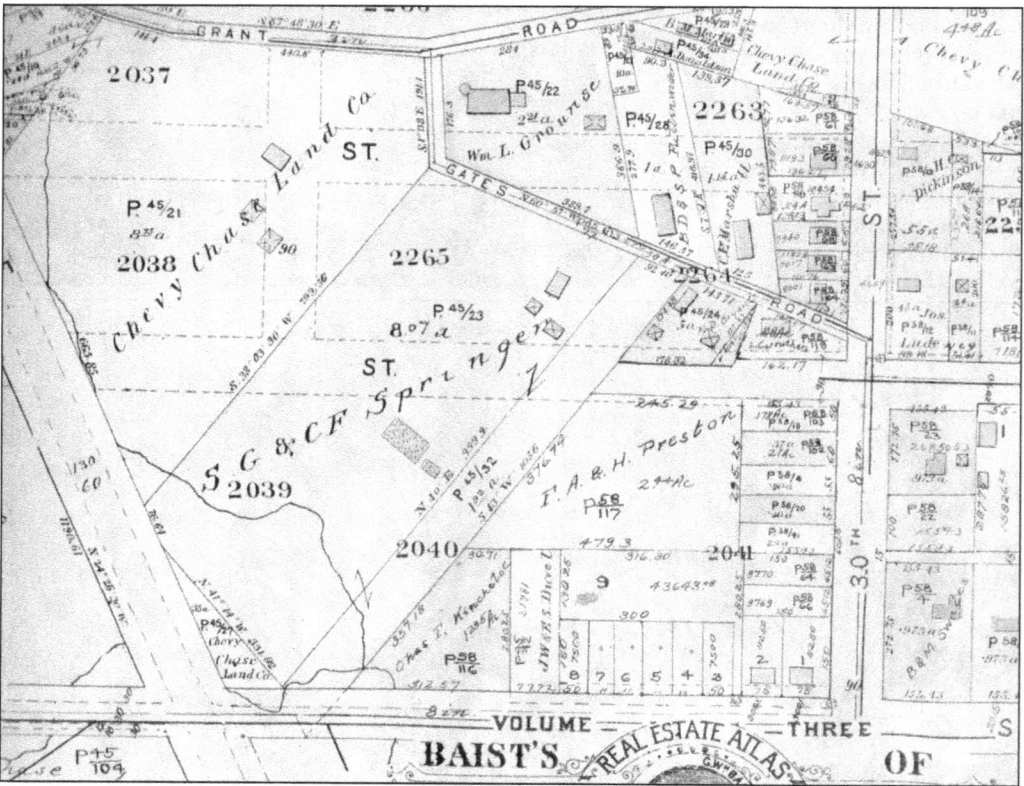

In 1949, developers Charles E. Smith and Morris Kanfer bought seven acres just north of the intersection of Connecticut Avenue and Albemarle Street known as the "old Springer tract." The developers originally planned to build a huge, 800-unit apartment building between Albemarle and Brandywine Streets. At the time, the House Public Works Committee was considering various plans for dispersal of federal offices to make them less vulnerable to nuclear attack, and Kanfer tried to convince them to lease space below the building for government offices and a bomb shelter. By 1951, he had given up this idea and went on to build two apartment houses, the Brandywine (1953) and Albemarle House (1958), both designed by the firm Corning and Moore. (Paul K. Williams Private Collection.)

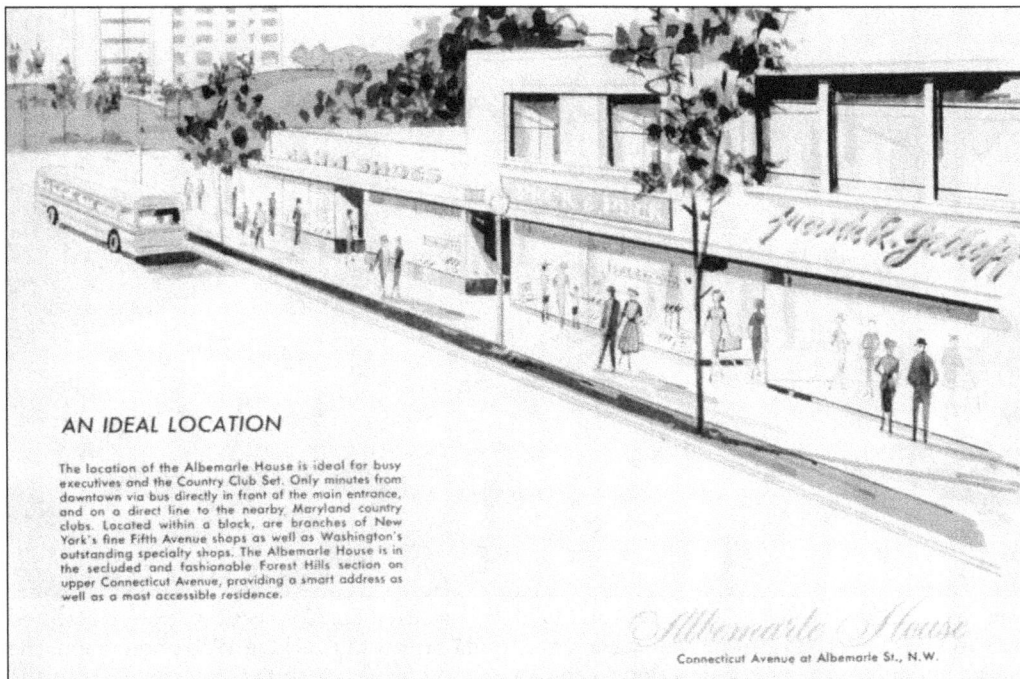

When the Albemarle House opened in the fall of 1958, it was touted as the epitome of elegance, including its "luxurious lobby, with its walnut paneling, polished marble and smart, modern decor." This page from a promotional brochure emphasizes both the convenience and the exclusivity of the area, and shows some of the stores that were located on Connecticut Avenue at the time. (James Goode Collection, HSW.)

By 1964, when Emil Press photographed the corner of Connecticut Avenue and Van Ness Street, this commercial strip was poised for a major change. All of the buildings shown here, except the liquor store and the Texaco gas station hidden beyond the Pontiac dealer, would be demolished and replaced, most of them by the new Van Ness Centre development. Flood Pontiac, which had two locations a block apart, lost its showroom in the 4300 block (the white building in the distance) and consolidated its business at 4217–4221 Connecticut, replacing the old building next to the liquor store with the present three-story structure. Founded by Everett Flood on Connecticut Avenue in 1933, the automobile dealership sold Pontiacs, Checker cabs, and even Rolls Royces for a while before closing in 1980. (Press Collection, HSW.)

Van Ness Centre was built between 1964 and 1970 on 18 acres east of Connecticut Avenue, bordered by Van Ness Street, Soapstone Valley Park, and Yuma Street. In this June 1966 photograph, the North building is under construction in the foreground, while the office complex rises in the background. Designed by Van Fossen Schwab and Shanti Singh Sukthankar, the Van Ness East building, farthest from Connecticut Avenue, was completed in 1964. The architectural firm Berla and Abel designed the other buildings in the complex; Robert I. Silverman developed the apartment buildings, while Milton and Howard Polinger and Stanley Zupnik built the office building. When the Van Ness North building was completed in 1967, Joseph Abel, one of the architects, moved into a three-bedroom apartment and lived there until his death in 1985. (HSW.)

The Van Ness Centre commercial building opened in 1967, with space for stores on the two lower levels and offices above. The upper floor of shops was converted to office space in 1983, and the entire building underwent a face-lift and reorganization of the retail space in 2005–2006. (MLK.)

In 1969, the National Bureau of Standards relocated the last of its offices to Gaithersburg, Maryland, and its former campus has been under development ever since. The old buildings did not all come down at once; Building Number 11, shown here, at the corner of Van Ness Street and Connecticut Avenue, was demolished in 1972. (MLK.)

In this aerial view dating from around 1980 and looking west over the Van Ness Centre complex, the buildings for the University of the District of Columbia are still under construction, and a few of the old National Bureau of Standards buildings remain across Van Ness Street. More change was coming in the form of the Metro subway stop, which opened on December 5, 1981, the third form of mass transit to carry riders along the Connecticut Avenue corridor since electric streetcars in the 1890s. (HSW.)

When Emil Press photographed the east side of Connecticut Avenue north of Fessenden Street in 1968, Safeway had been there for almost 30 years and Higger's Drugstore, next door, for 38 years. Although anchored by service stations on three corners, the 5000 block of Connecticut continued to be dominated by businesses that served the neighborhood: groceries, drugstores, hardware stores, repairmen, liquor stores, bakeries and gourmet shops, restaurants, hairdressers, and dry cleaners. Samuel Higger moved into 5017 Connecticut Avenue in August 1930 and had expanded into the store at 5015 as well by the time he sold the business to Leon Drapkin in 1969. When Safeway closed at 5013 Connecticut in 1976, Drapkin moved the drugstore into that much larger space. Drapkin sold Higger's in 1979 to Edward Sandel, who continued the store's long tradition of personalized service until forced by price competition from the big drugstore chains to close in 1996. The space is now occupied by CVS. (Press Collection, HSW.)

Kay Walters

Cafe Burgundy

5031 CONNECTICUT AVE., N.W
(at Nebraska Ave.)
WASHINGTON 8, D. C.
EMerson 2-7045

FAMOUS FOR

"EXCELLENT FOOD"
•
FINE WINES
•
COCKTAILS

Cafe Burgundy became a popular neighborhood restaurant almost as soon as it opened in 1954. Although the *Washington Post* restaurant critic in 1968 noted that its "claim to be of French descent is questionable," he complimented the appealing warmth of the room, where artificial grapes overflowed the ceiling lamps and booths lined the walls. The restaurant served a devoted following until 1990. (Jerry A. McCoy Postcard Collection.)

Three

DOMESTIC ARCHITECTURE
BY BARBARA D. BATES

There is a range of architectural styles reflected in Forest Hills, from the early homes to postmodern, contemporary, and environmental designs. Dwellings here consist of single, semi-detached, row, and apartment houses. While much has been written on apartments, little has been published on the other houses and the remarkable architects who designed them. This chapter provides information on these extant treasures.

Several early homes built in the 19th century remain, including those that belonged to the Peirce family, discussed in Chapter One. The Peirce-Klingle Mansion (Linnaean Hill, 1823), at 3545 Williamsburg Lane, was the home of Isaac Peirce's son, Joshua, who operated a nursery and arboretum on the site. A farmhouse built in 1855 once fronted Grant Road; in 1927, when the address was changed to 3039 Davenport Street, architect Eimer Cappelman made significant modifications to the property, encasing the original frame house in brick. The Owl's Nest, built in 1897, is discussed in Chapter Four.

Ten single houses around Grant Road and on Albemarle Street and 12 semi-detached houses in Forest Hills date back to the first decade of the 20th century. The Arts and Crafts home at 2909 Brandywine Street was built in 1903 and designed by Andrew C. Plant Jr. Another dwelling, now located at 3239 Davenport Street, was built about the same time for florist John R. Morgan Jr. Originally located at 4801 Connecticut Avenue, it was moved to its present location in 1931.

Other early houses in Forest Hills include 4630 Thirtieth Street, built in 1906 and designed by John Simpson Jr.; 4629 Thirtieth Street, built in 1907 and designed by the Keith and Company firm; 4609 Thirtieth Street, built that same year and designed by the owner, Joseph Ludewig; and 3011 Gates Road, built about 1907. Three houses designed by Arthur B. Heaton in slightly varying styles were built in 1909 at what are now 4501 and 4535 Thirtieth Street and 2955 Albemarle Street. The six pairs of semi-detached houses at 2963–2941 Tilden Street were built in 1906 as part of Fernwood Heights, the first subdivision in Forest Hills by William H. Germann, the architect, owner, and builder.

Six single-family houses and 19 row houses that were built in the second decade of the 20th century remain in Forest Hills. Lawyer Fred B. Rhodes hired the Speiden and Speiden firm to build two houses in the Colonial Revival style on Albemarle Street—3006 in 1910 and 3000 in 1920. The deep ravines and rolling terrain indicate the challenges met by the architects and builders of these homes.

Another early house in Forest Hills was built in 1912 in a neoclassical style at 2901 Grant Road for Dr. Charles W. Richardson, who had hired the Marsh and Peter firm. By the 1950s, Vespucci V. Petrone owned the estate and subdivided the property into lots, creating Ellicott Terrace. The address was changed to 2907 and 2901 Ellicott Terrace for the two original buildings, and seven houses were then built from 1955 to 1962 on the new lots.

In 1913, the firm Hornblower and Marshall designed a Dutch Colonial house for Mrs. Edward F. Morgan at 3303 Fessenden Street. In 1917, the house at 4620 Thirtieth Street, designed by Hanson M. Cronise, was built for Treasury employee Lawrence J. Johnson. In 1918, the house built at 3105 Ellicott Street was designed by B. Frank Meyers for eye physician Dr. Carl Henning. Six row houses at 2930–2920 Upton Street were built in 1915, and three row houses between 2936 and 2932 Upton Street were built in 1916, designed by George N. Ray; the latter are attached to six row houses built at 2920–2930 Upton Street built in 1915, designed by Frank Russell White. Four row houses were built at 2927–2921 Tilden Street a year later, designed by Matthew G. Lepley.

As a testament to their fine design, many of the estates now serve as residences for foreign ambassadors, as discussed in Chapter Nine. Others have contributed to the modern architectural design, such as the residence of the State of Kuwait at 2940 Tilden Street, designed by Van Fossen Schwab and built in 1965. Others include homes now owned by the governments of the Kingdom of the Netherlands at 2501 Upton Street, built in 1924 and designed by Arthur B. Heaton; the Republic of Indonesia at 2700 Tilden Street, built in 1925 and designed by Sonneman and Justement; and the Democratic Republic of Congo at 4001 Linnean Avenue, built in 1940 and designed by Porter and Lockie.

While a larger proportion of the houses in Forest Hills date back to the 1920s and 1930s, more were built in the 1950s and 1960s than in any other decades. Prominent architects have been hired across the decades to design individual plans to suit the aesthetics of the period. Interestingly the last open tract to be developed was that of Lenore Lane in the 1980s. Construction has continued into the 21st century, blending the old with the new and fitting into the contours of the landscape, with work under way along many streets in the neighborhood.

Today Forest Hills serves as a showcase for many well-known architects, some of whom also designed homes for themselves, including Harvey P. Baxter (2928 Ellicott Street, 1939); Edmund W. Dreyfuss (4528 Twenty-Eighth Street, 1949); Charles F. D. Egbert (2801 Davenport Street, 1970); Stanley I. Hallet (4542 Twenty-Eighth Street, 1996); and Travis L. Price III (2805 Chesterfield Place, 2004). Many other architects known at this time have worked in Forest Hills are too numerous to mention in this chapter. Examples of 22 architects have been selected to reflect the range of styles of over 11 decades of residential development.

The six pairs of semi-detached houses from 2963 to 2941 Tilden Street, shown, were built in 1906 by architect, owner, and builder William H. Germann (1857–1944). These are the only remaining early structures built in the subdivision of Fernwood Heights, laid out and recorded on March 25, 1902, by Edward J. Stellwagen, vice-president of the Chevy Chase Land Company at that time. Lots were located on Connecticut Avenue between Quincy (Tilden Street), Randolph (Upton Street), and Shepherd Streets (Van Ness Street) and over these streets to Twenty-Ninth Street. The last dwellings to be built on the lots were three pairs of semi-detached houses on Tilden Street and four pairs of semi-detached houses on Upton Street in 1953, followed by one pair in 1956. (Photograph by Paul K. Williams.)

This house at 2909 Brandywine Street was built in 1903. The architect, Andrew Clinton Plant Jr. (1875–1944), designed this house in the Arts and Crafts style. While he worked on no other houses in Forest Hills, he did design a frame dwelling in Chevy Chase, a pair of semi-detached brick houses in LeDroit Park, and three structures on E and F Streets, NE, between 1902 and 1908. He served as an architectural draftsman with the Bureau of Yards and Docks, Department of the Navy, and then as architect for the Departments of the Treasury and Navy. (Photograph by Barbara D. Bates.)

The house seen here at 3303 Fessenden Street was built in 1913. The architect, James Rush Marshall (1851–1927) of the firm Hornblower and Marshall, designed this house in the Dutch Colonial style. He continued to practice under the firm's name after the death of his partner in 1908, working primarily on residential or remodeling commissions. The firm was founded in 1883 and is known for the design of its residences as well as such buildings as the National Museum of Natural History of the Smithsonian Institution and the Army and Navy Club. (Photograph by Barbara D. Bates.)

This house at 3000 Albemarle Street was constructed in 1920 and was designed in the Colonial Revival style by architect Albert Speiden (1868–1933). He continued to practice under the firm's name, Speiden and Speiden, after the death of his partner and brother. The firm was founded in 1896 and designed many buildings throughout Washington, D.C., including two residences in the Kalorama Historic District. This was their second home in Forest Hills; both were designed for Fred Burnett Rhodes on Albemarle Street. Albert Speiden is recognized for his buildings in Manassas, Virginia, that are included in the Manassas Historic District. (Photograph by Barbara D. Bates.)

This house at 3020 Albemarle Street was built in 1924. The architect, Horace W. Peasley (1884–1959), designed this house in the Mediterranean style. This is one of 10 houses that he designed in Forest Hills between 1922 and 1941, including the home for Charles H. Tompkins near the remains of Civil War–era Battery Terrill; built in 1925, it became the property of the government of Peru in 1944 and serves as their embassy residence today. Peasley established his own practice in 1918. He is considered the principal architect of Meridian Hill Park (completed in 1930) and the Marine Corps Memorial grounds, dedicated in 1954. (Photograph by Barbara D. Bates.)

The house at 3126 Ellicott Street, seen here, was built in 1928 in the Colonial Revival style and was designed by architect Arthur B. Heaton (1875–1951). This is one of 10 houses that he designed in Forest Hills between 1909 and 1932, including the home for Clyde B. Asher, built in 1924; it became the property of the government of the Kingdom of the Netherlands in 1960 and serves as the residence of a Dutch official today. Heaton established his own practice in 1900. He also designed the Methodist Home of D.C. at 4901 Connecticut Avenue, which was dedicated in 1926, and the historic Park and Shop shopping center in Cleveland Park, built in 1930. (Photograph by Barbara D. Bates.)

Built in 1930 at 4545 Linnean Avenue, this house was designed by architect James E. Cooper (1877–1930) in the Tudor style. This is one of five houses that he designed in Forest Hills between 1927 and 1930. These include the stone dwelling built for Sen. Thomas P. Gore in 1925, which was sold to the Malaya government (now the Federation of Malaysia) in 1957 for the first ambassador's residence, and the stone dwelling built for Joseph Sanders in 1927, which was sold to the Czechoslovak Socialist Republic (now the Czech Republic) in 1961 and continues to serve as the ambassador's residence. Cooper also designed Cleveland Park (1924–1925) on Porter Street, considered a forerunner of garden apartments, and Foxhall Village, opened in 1930. (Photograph by Barbara D. Bates.)

The house at 2944 Brandywine Street was built in 1931. Called the Elmhurst by Sears, Roebuck and Company, this is one of three Sears houses in Forest Hills, all located on Brandywine Street. The second, located at 2908 Brandywine Street, was built in 1927, and the design is the Puritan. The third house, located at 2965 Brandywine Street, was built in 1926, and the original design has not been determined. The Sears Elmhurst model first appeared in the 1931 catalog as house number 3300. It was purchased that same year and constructed at 2944 Brandywine Street for Internal Revenue Service agent Joe N. McCollum and his wife, Ruth. (http://www.SearsArchives.com.)

This house at 2847 Allendale Place was constructed in 1934. Designed by Claude N. Norton (1889–1957) in a Colonial Revival variant style, it is one of 27 single-family and row houses that he designed in Forest Hills between 1923 and 1934. His works in 1923 were the four two-story, brick row houses located at 4035–4029 Connecticut Avenue in the Fernwood Heights area for owner and builder H. P. Huddleson. His last two houses in Forest Hills were those on Allendale Place for owner and builder Alfred T. Newbold. (Photograph by Barbara D. Bates.)

Architect Edwin A. Weihe (1907–1994) designed this house built in 1940, in the Colonial Revival style at 3219 Chesapeake Street. It is one of two houses that he designed in Forest Hills. He entered private practice in 1939, later founding the Weihe Partnership. After service in World War II, he became known for designing large office and apartment buildings. These include many of the buildings along the K Street corridor, such as 1701 K Street, 1001 Connecticut Avenue, and 1666 K Street, and apartment complexes such as 4200 Cathedral Avenue and the Crystal House and River House in Arlington, Virginia. (Photograph by Barbara D. Bates.)

This house at 3108 Fessenden Street, built in 1942, was designed by Joseph A. Parks (1889–1971) in the Colonial Revival style. This is one of 10 houses that he designed in Forest Hills between 1940 and 1942; eight of these were in Ellicott Hills for owner and builder James E. Schwab, who planned a community of walled gardens. Parks was a partner in Parks and Baxter from 1926 to 1931. His firm also designed a house in Forest Hills and is recognized for its work on Tilden Gardens apartments (1927–1929) with Harry L. Edwards in an English Tudor Revival style. (Photograph by Barbara D. Bates.)

Architect Walter D. Byrd (1919–1974) designed this house in 1951 in the modern style for David Lloyd and Carmen Kreeger at 3201 Fessenden Street. The California redwood and Stoney Hurst ledge rock on the exterior come into the interior, reflecting a Japanese influence. Byrd served as a designer and/or draftsman in Michigan and Washington, D.C., before becoming a registered architecture in the District of Columbia in 1950. By December 1958, however, he had relocated to Florida. (Photograph by Paul K. Williams.)

COVENANTS BY MARGERY ELFIN

Forest Hills has a reputation for demographic diversity. It was a pioneer for neighborhoods "west of the Park" in opening housing to Jews, blacks, and other minority groups who had long been excluded from other nearby neighborhoods by means of restrictive covenants. Whether this can be explained by the relatively late population growth in Forest Hills or by the low percentage of large-scale housing development, as opposed to individual homeowners, is problematic. Whatever the reasons, by the 1960s, Forest Hills became known to locals as "Hanukkah Heights," because it had become the residence of choice for many Jewish families. Restrictive covenants are agreements inserted into real-estate contracts that enforce segregation, usually by religion and race, on the parties to the contract. The seller agrees not to sell to a member of a designated group. The point of these covenants was to maintain "lily white" neighborhoods. They were commonplace until a series of postwar court decisions made the practice unenforceable. Developers and real-estate agencies collaborated to keep them viable so long as they went unchallenged. As late as 1948, the words "no colored" still appeared in real-estate advertising. An article in *Commentary* magazine of May 1947, "Homes for Aryans Only," was a plea for public education to end the practice of restrictive covenants. The use of the word "Aryan" is telling, only two years after the defeat of Hitler. Coming home to a housing shortage after World War II, Jewish and African American veterans were met with the exclusionary housing policies of the time. There were lawsuits filed all over the country. One of the cases was brought in the Washington suburb of Bethesda, in a neighborhood called Bannockburn Heights. A Jewish man, Aaron Tushin, had bought a home at 6918 Wilson Lane. The deed to the home included a restrictive covenant, which the seller ignored. However nine residents of the neighborhood filed suit to force him to move. The precedent setting case was *Shelley v. Kraemer* (334 US1), 1948, in which the Supreme Court changed the prior rule of law applicable to these covenants. It held that such agreements are not invalid so long as they are voluntary, but they do not compel compliance. A companion case, *Hurd v. Hodge*, held that the enforcement by the federal courts of restrictive covenants in the District of Columbia was a denial of due process of law guaranteed by the Fifth Amendment. In 1963, the court applied the Shelley doctrine to sit-in demonstrations at segregated lunch counters. Negro patrons refused to leave and were arrested for trespass. The arrests were held to be enforcements of the community segregation policy and a denial of equal protection. This ruling was very important to the notion of restrictive covenants. The court concluded that "because of the race or color of these petitioners they have been denied rights of ownership or occupancy enjoyed as a matter of course by other citizens of different race or color." As late as 1965, segregated housing as a violation of a fundamental human rights was addressed: "Human rights all too often include the unrealized right to choose a place of residence and to purchase property, which clashes with the not unlimited rights of those who own property in the desired location." Bulletin #32 April 1965 by the National Conference of Christians and Jews. (Graphic by Gregory J. Alexander.)

This house, built in 1951, at 2604 Tilden Place, with later additions was designed by Arthur H. Keyes Jr. (1917–). This home is located among others designed in the Modern style in the 1950s by such architects as Charles M. Goodman and Nicholas Satterlee. Keyes was a founder of the firms initially named Keyes, Smith, Satterlee, and Lethbridge in 1950; it has been reorganized a number of times since and is known today as Keyes, Condon, and Florance. Over the decades, his firm have been associated with modern apartment and office complexes such as Tiber Island SW in 1965 and 2401 Pennsylvania Avenue NW in 1991. (Photograph by Barbara D. Bates.)

Architect Leon Brown (1907–1992) designed this house at 4500 Thirty-First Street built in 1958 in the Modern style with influences from Japanese architecture. This is one of more than 12 single-family houses that he designed in Forest Hills between 1949 and 1961. Brown resided at 4158 Linnean Avenue for several years and was a professor of architecture at Howard University from 1947 to 1972. He founded his own firm in 1946, which was the first to provide an integrated setting for some of his students. He later worked as partner in Brown and Smull (1948); Brown and Wright (1950–1962, 1970–1980); Brown, Chapman, Miller, Wright (1962–1963); and Brown, Wright, Mano (1968–1970). The work of his firms included housing projects and the Embassy of Ghana Chancery in 1974 on International Drive. (Photograph by Paul K. Williams.)

This house at 2901 Fessenden Street, built in 1962, was designed by architect Cloethiel Woodard Smith (1910–1992) in the Modern style for Stanley Bender, treasurer of the Blake Construction Company. Smith was a partner in several local firms before forming her own in 1963. Also an urban planner, she worked on the master plan for the Southwest Urban Renewal Project and Waterfront. Her firm has been associated with residential and office construction such as 1100 Connecticut Avenue and Blake Building (1964–1966) and Washington Square (1984) and Harbour Square apartments and townhouses (1963–1966) in Southwest. She was also a founding trustee of the National Building Museum. (Photograph by Barbara D. Bates.)

This house at 3003 Audubon Terrace, built between 1965 and 1967, was designed by well-known architect Hugh Newell Jacobsen (1929–) in the Modern style. He established his own practice in 1958, and his work has included mostly single-family homes known for their use of interconnecting rooms or pavilions, such as the Dreier-Barton House (1977), and institutional structures such as the Georgetown University Village B Student Housing (1984); expansion of the Cafritz House (1965); renovation of the Renwick Gallery of the Smithsonian Institution (1967–1972); and the addition of office spaces under the West Terrace of the United States Capitol (1993). (Photograph by Paul K. Williams.)

Architect Richard J. Neutra (1892–1970) designed this house built in 1968 at 3005 Audubon Terrace. The original owners sought out this master architect of the International style for their home, and he personally selected the lot for them in Forest Hills. This is the only home that he designed in Washington, D.C., and it is his last work. Architect Heather Willson Cass (1947–) designed the 1992 addition. Born in Vienna, Austria, Neutra came to the United States in 1923 and in 1925 moved to Los Angeles, California, where he established his practice. He was a partner with Robert Alexander from 1949 to 1958 and with his son in Richard and Dion Neutra Associates from 1965 to 1970. His works include private residences, many located in California, and public buildings such as the Los Angeles Hall of Records with Alexander in 1962. (Photograph by Paul K. Williams.)

The house seen here at 2801 Davenport Street was constructed in 1970. It was designed by Charles F. D. Egbert (1932–) as his own home in a Modern style that anticipates the Postmodern style, with its silo-sized column as a central feature. He founded his firm Charles F. D. Egbert in 1964. His principal works in the area include residences in Tulip Hill and Bethesda, Maryland, and Reston, Virginia. He was associate architect on the RAD-MAT Electronic Radiation Facility in Gaithersburg, Maryland (1969). (Photograph by Paul K. Williams.)

Pioneering owners designed this house as an earth-sheltered home at 2830 Upton Street, built in 1981. It is a passive solar house and has a green roof. Today green roofs are recognized as a major component of the green infrastructure and a complement to trees in creating healthy environments. Benefits to the community include improved air quality, reduction in storm water runoff, and cooler summer temperatures. The government of the District of Columbia cohosted the Third Annual Greening Rooftops for Sustainable Communities Conference in May 2005, indicating a commitment to this technology in creating a green vision for the city. (Photograph by Barbara D. Bates.)

This house at 4205 Linnean Avenue, built in 1983, was designed by Joseph E. Wnuk (1943–) in the Postmodern style. It is located among a cluster of 14 Contemporary-style homes built between 1980 and 1989 in an area that has been referred to as the "Street of Dreams" of both owners and architects. He was a recipient of the First Annual Mayor's Award for Architecture in 1986 for this house. Wnuk founded his firm in 1979 and was joined by Stephen Spurlock to form Wnuk Spurlock. In 1999 they were partners in McMurray, Wnuk, and Spurlock. Their works have also included commercial and institutional structures, as well as educational and cultural facilities such as the Liz Lerman Dance Exchange in Takoma Park, Maryland. (Photograph by H. Hambright.)

The house built at 4542 Twenty-Eighth Street was built in 1996. Architect Stanley Ira Hallet (1941–) designed his own home in the Contemporary style with influences from Afghanistan architecture. He was a Fulbright-Hayes Lecturer at the University of Kabul in 1971 and coauthored a book with Rafi Samizay titled *Traditional Architecture of Afghanistan*, which was published in 1980. He has served as a professor of architecture at the University of Utah, where he formed the partnership Hallet, Hermanson, and Associates (1977–82). He has served as professor of architecture at the Catholic University of America School of Architecture and Planning since 1986 and as dean from 1991–1996, with an expertise in Islamic architecture. He became an associate with Roger K. Lewis and Associates in 1996. (Photograph courtesy Stanley Hallet.)

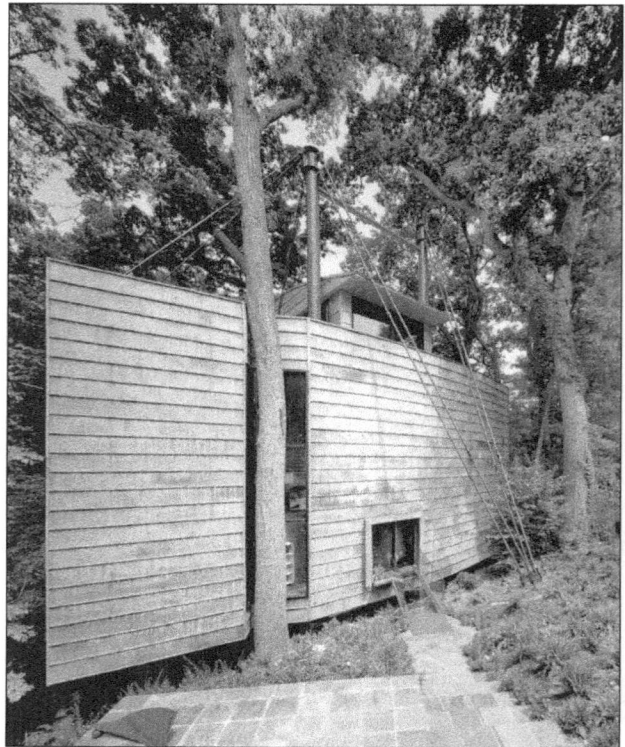

This house at 2805 Chesterfield Place, built in 2004, was designed by Travis L. Price III (1949–) as his family home in the Contemporary style. Copper-clad from the front, the house viewed from the back along Davenport Street shows the glass-enclosed levels as they reach down into the steep hillside. He is a solar architect and formerly worked on renovating buildings in New York City for use of solar energy. He was the first coordinator of the Solar Program of the Tennessee Valley Authority. His current firm, Travis Price Architects, continues to do pioneering work in passive solar design for residential, institutional, and commercial construction and renovation. (Photograph by Kenneth M. Wyner.)

Four

THE OWL'S NEST

By Gary Stevens and Judith H. Robinson

William L. Crounse, a prominent journalist and trade association representative, hired local architect Appleton P. Clark Jr. to design and construct a "modern country dwelling," according to an *Evening Star* newspaper account on April 3, 1897, in what was then the outskirts of Washington. The house, which became known as the Owl's Nest, is located on high ground at 3130 Gates Road. Today the estate retains much of its original landscape and exterior design and is the only private home in Forest Hills designated as a local District of Columbia landmark.

Built in 1897, the Owl's Nest is an unusual and skillful adaptation of shingle-style architecture. The variety of surface textures is complemented by an equally rich diversity of shapes, including rugged stone pillars and arches, and projecting elements such as dormers, oriels, and a porte cochere. The picturesque appearance of the house is augmented by its landscape setting, at the top of a gentle hill planted with mature trees of a variety of species, including several giant oak trees more than 150 years old. The dwelling was later expanded by adding a servant's wing in 1912–1913, also designed by Clark.

The Owl's Nest stands out distinctly from its surroundings due to its age and its unique architectural character. The Owl's Nest is located on a large lot nearly two acres in size. The northern boundary is formed by a fragment of Grant Road, while Gates Road on the south side of the estate leads to the semi-circular entrance drive that has become the main access point to the house. On April 3, 1897, the following item appeared in the "Real Estate Gossip" column in the *Evening Star* newspaper: "A modern country dwelling is being erected on the property of Wm L. Crounse near Connecticut avenue extended, about the Military and Gates Roads. The house is to be of stone and wood, two stories with cellar. A. P. Clark Jr., is the architect, and Galloway & Son are the builders."

Crounse obviously intended the Owl's Nest to reflect and enhance his prestige as a prominent member of Washington society. Prior to the construction of the Owl's Nest, suburban living in Northwest Washington was presaged by the construction of summerhouses and country estates for the wealthy outside the traditional city limits. Earlier country estates in the Cleveland Park area to the south and west of Forest Hills included Woodley, built by Philip Barton Key about 1800; the Highlands, built in the 1820s; and Springland, built in the 1840s. Pres. Grover Cleveland remodeled an old farm house called Red Tops for summer use in 1886.

The appeal of the suburban lifestyle in Washington was described in the May 2, 1896, edition of the *Evening Star* newspaper, published just a year prior to the construction of the Owl's Nest. It reads:

> As it is well known, the country about this city possesses many natural advantages, and there are some portions which, in point of beauty of scenery, [are] said to be superior to that which can be found in a vicinity of any other city in the country. . . . One feature, of course, which draws people to the country is the spacious building sites which can be secured for considerably less money than the average building lot in the city . . . the average man or woman likes to live reasonably near a stretch of green grass, dotted here and there with trees and shrubbery.

Appleton Clark was one of the most prominent and prolific architects working in Washington at the time. A graduate of Central High School in 1883, his 60-year career included the building of virtually every type of structure, encompassing banks, apartment buildings, churches, residences, institutions, and office buildings, in many of the popular architectural styles of the day. Most of his work utilized the Classical Revival styles that were popular at the time; however the rustic shingle style of the Owl's Nest seems an unusual departure for Clark and represents an aspect of his work that was either unrecognized at the time or rare, perhaps unique.

Crounse continued to live in the Owl's Nest until he sold it in 1927 to Cmdr. Fritz Louis Sandos, a Louisiana native and veteran of the Spanish-American War. According to his obituary, Commander Sandos "was in command of the landing party which captured the enemy fort at Mantazas, Cuba, and raised the American flag over it." The 1930 census records that Sandos lived there with his wife, Anna, twin daughters, Nancy and Priscilla, and two live-in servants. In 1939, the house was rented to the Baron Herve de Gruben, a counselor to the Belgian Embassy, who lived there until about 1941. In 1947, the house was sold to Alvin Brown, a local real-estate developer, who lived in the house until 2001, when it was sold to a private school.

Plans by the school to raze the house and build a three-story elementary school were opposed by many neighbors who formed the Forest Hills Neighborhood Alliance, which secured landmark designation for the property to prevent demolition. The school sold the estate to AB Urban Development, which undertook some much-needed repairs. The renovation-in-progress was purchased by the Donatelli and Klein Company in early 2006, with continued plans for its preservation as a private residence. The future of the Owl's Nest as a unique landmark feature of Forest Hills now seems secure.

This is the earliest known sketch of the Owl's Nest, one of several drawn of prominent country houses on the outskirts of Washington during the early 20th century. At the time, the house would have been surrounded by acres of undeveloped land and forest. Despite development in the surrounding area, it remains today on one of the largest lots in Forest Hills. (HSW.)

Appleton P. Clark designed the Owl's Nest in 1897, somewhat early in a career that spanned over 60 years. His best-known buildings in Washington include the *Washington Post* building (Romanesque Revival style, 1893; demolished 1954), the Presidential Apartments (Beaux Arts style, 1922), and the Foundry United Methodist Church (1903–1904). In the late 1890s, Clark was in high demand as an architect, and his name was mentioned in the real-estate column of the *Washington Star* newspaper on an almost weekly basis. (Kelsey and Associates, Inc.)

The west facade of the Owl's Nest is the original "front" of the house. It is defined by four primary elements: a stone turret, an entrance arch, a hip-roof dormer, and a porte cochere. This ensemble of architectural elements arising out of a grove of trees would have left a lasting impression on visitors to Crounse's new home, as it does to this day. (Photograph by Paul K. Williams.)

The south facade, which is the current front of the Owl's Nest, is informally organized and is even more indicative of the shingle style. The first story, including the two supports of the porte cochere, is clad in stone, with the exception of an addition that extends to the east that is clad in wood shingles. Three low windows at ground level light the basement. These have rough stone jack arches at the lintels, and at the first-story level to the east of the porte cochere is a tripartite window. The second and third stories are shingled, with a stone chimney. (Photograph by Paul K. Williams.)

The simple stone mantel over the living room fireplace is devoid of detail except for the inscription *Quod Sors Feret Feremus*, a quote from the Latin poet Terence, which in translation reads "Whatever fate brings to us we shall meet with equanimity." (Photograph by Paul K. Williams.)

The stained glass image of an owl's head is a colorful and playful element that lends a touch of humor to the imposing structure of the Owl's Nest. It is located on the first landing of the main staircase. (Photograph by Paul K. Williams.)

The pillar at the original entrance to the property on the west bears a barely legible description announcing the Owl's Nest to visitors. Today it is located along rarely utilized Grant Road, a new driveway to the south having replaced the old entrance several decades ago. (Photograph by Paul K. Williams.)

Bold and romantic architectural elements were worked into the roof details of the Owl's Nest, including an unusual curved slate roof over the front doorway. Metal brackets set into the slate prevent snow and ice from sliding off the roof during inclement weather. (Photograph by Paul K. Williams.)

Five

THE SCIENTIFIC COMMUNITY

BY MARGERY ELFIN AND ANNE ROLLINS

In 1901, an act of Congress created the National Bureau of Standards (NBS), which had its origins as the Office of Weights and Measures, a division of the Treasury Department created in 1867 in response to increasing industrialization. Because of the new agency's expanded role, it needed space for a complex of buildings to house its growing staff and the employees' myriad experiments. The first director, Samuel Stratton, who served from 1901 until 1922, located eight acres overlooking Connecticut Avenue at Tilden Street, which the government bought for $25,000 from the Chevy Chase Land Company.

Over time, the NBS expanded, acquiring more parcels of land, eventually totaling 89 buildings on 70 acres along the west side of Connecticut Avenue from roughly Van Ness Street to Yuma Street today. The largest employer in Forest Hills, it was mandated with testing new materials for future manufacturing and consumer consumption as well as establishing a wide variety of standards for measuring heat, fuel, distances, and the inherent qualities of newly developing materials at the time.

When the NBS moved to Gaithersburg, Maryland, in 1968, its buildings were demolished; they were replaced by the International Center, which would eventually include 20 chanceries and the Intelsat Corporation. Remaining land was used for the Washington Technical Institute, which later merged with D.C. Teachers College and the Federal City College to become the University of the District of Columbia. In 1988, the NBS was renamed the National Institute of Standards and Technology (NIST).

Radio work was at the heart of the NBS research. In 1904, Dr. Louis W. Austin began to investigate the application of radiotelegraphy for the navy. The NBS received $10,000 in 1915 for the "investigation and standardization of methods and instruments employed in radio communication." Many residents worked at the NBS as physicists in radio technology and provided a textbook that Thomas Edison called "the greatest book on the subject that I have ever read."

It was a relaxed workplace despite the seriousness of the research. A personal memoir of Jacob Rabinow, one of the young scientists at the NBS, illustrates this perfectly in his monograph *Inventing for Fun and Profit* published by San Francisco Press in 1990:

We worked on many things. Bill McLean and I actually designed rockets that we used to fire in the "forest" north of Van Ness Street, where the UDC stands today. We would load the rockets ourselves and test them there among the trees. One of them got away from me and went upward instead of horizontally. I was afraid that it would go over the trees and hit the Hot Shoppe Restaurant on Connecticut Avenue and Van Ness, and I said to myself, "Oh, oh, we're going to shell that building and it's going to be very embarrassing." There was no explosive in the shell, but it would still have made a large hole in the roof of the restaurant. Fortunately, it hit the top of a tall tree, bounced off, and the Hot Shoppe never knew how close it was to being in the [second world] war.

By the 1930s, the NBS was active in working on radio beacons that would help pilots find their positions in flight. This work directed by Harry Diamond beginning in 1927. His refinements enabled the first blind landing of an airplane entirely by radio guidance. Diamond and his colleagues did valuable research in developing the proximity fuse, a tiny radio sending and receiving device described later by the War Department as "one of the outstanding scientific developments of World War II . . . second only to the atomic bomb" in importance. The Diamond Laboratories, now part of the Department of the Army, are named in his honor.

The Carnegie Institution of Washington established two scientific research laboratories in Forest Hills. Both the Geophysical Laboratory and the Department of Terrestrial Magnetism were carefully sited far enough from Connecticut Avenue to avoid vibrations from the streetcar line and on rock formations that did not have strong magnetic fields, either of which would have affected the delicate experiments in the laboratories. The laboratory on Upton Street was completed in 1907 and concentrated on the study of the physics and chemistry of the earth's interior and mantle, including such specialties as petrology, seismology, volcanology, and isotopic geochemistry. Important research into the creation of a metal from super-cooled and pressurized hydrogen was also accomplished. In 1990, it relocated to the campus of the Department of Terrestrial Magnetism, and the former building is now the Levine School of Music.

The Department of Terrestrial Magnetism (DTM) moved into its building on Broad Branch Road in 1914. Creating a map of the earth's geomagnetic field dominated the institution's earliest activities, with later research in such areas as the ionosphere, radio waves, and physics. By the 1930s and 1940s, the DTM was a world-class center for nuclear physics, building a succession of increasingly powerful Van de Graaff generators and a large cyclotron on the grounds. In January 1939, in response to rumors of uranium fission by German physicists, Carnegie scientists demonstrated fission for a conference of leading American physicists, creating a sensation in the press. After the war, DTM was noted for its work in molecular biology.

This is a map that shows how the National Bureau of Standards gradually increased its land holdings in Forest Hills. From the first purchase of eight acres in 1901 until the last purchase in 1942, the campus grew to more than 70 acres. (MLK.)

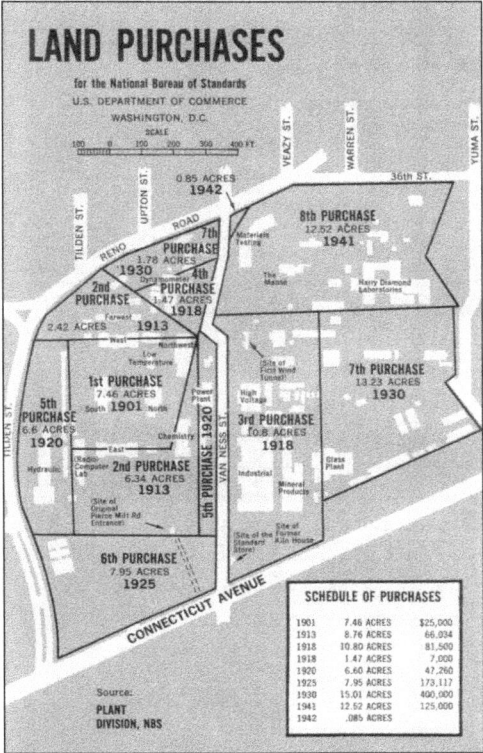

LAND PURCHASES
for the National Bureau of Standards
U.S. DEPARTMENT OF COMMERCE
WASHINGTON, D.C.
SCALE

0.85 ACRES
1942

7th PURCHASE
1.78 ACRES
1930

2nd PURCHASE
2.42 ACRES 1913

4th PURCHASE
1.47 ACRES
1918

8th PURCHASE
12.52 ACRES
1941

Harry Diamond Laboratories

1st PURCHASE
7.46 ACRES
1901

7th PURCHASE
13.23 ACRES
1930

5th PURCHASE
6.6 ACRES
1920

3rd PURCHASE
10.8 ACRES
1918

2nd PURCHASE
6.34 ACRES
1913

6th PURCHASE
7.95 ACRES
1925

CONNECTICUT AVENUE

Source:
PLANT DIVISION, NBS

SCHEDULE OF PURCHASES		
1901	7.46 ACRES	$25,000
1913	8.76 ACRES	66,034
1918	10.80 ACRES	81,500
1918	1.47 ACRES	7,000
1920	6.60 ACRES	47,260
1925	7.95 ACRES	173,117
1930	15.01 ACRES	400,000
1941	12.52 ACRES	125,000
1942	.085 ACRES	

This picture shows a group of gentlemen attending the laying of the cornerstone for the new Physical Laboratory at the NBS in 1903. The campus would eventually grow to house nearly 90 major brick buildings and laboratories. (Photograph by George Alexander, LOC.)

The second director of the NBS, George K. Burgess, was a graduate of both MIT and the Sorbonne in France and had previously been the chief of metallurgy at the NBS. He took the position as director on April 21, 1923. (LOC.)

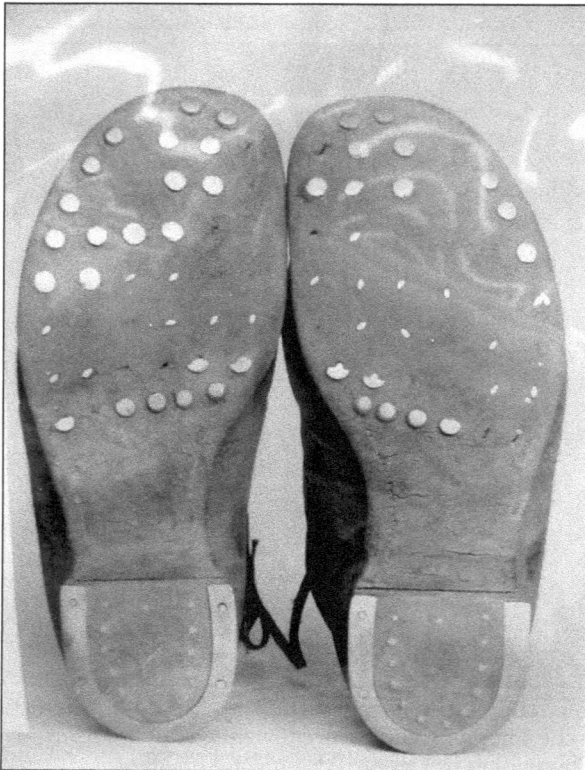

Contrary to preconception, the experiments at the NBS were not always complicated. One performed during the Great Depression was used to determine the value of the hobnail in preserving shoe leather. The shoe soles seen in this picture were subject to wear similar to that occurring in 90 days of actual use, and shows that the leather was barely worn, while the hobs are only partially worn off. (LOC.)

Harry Diamond was a young physicist who came to the National Bureau of Standards in 1927. He was recognized as an impressive talent by his colleagues and went on to do very important war work in the development of the proximity fuse. According to a history of the NBS, the "burst" of scientific accomplishment in World War II changed the course of research from its early orientation toward industry to science. Norman Kiess, a resident of Forest Hills since his birth in 1930, remembers a neighborhood where many scientists who worked at the National Bureau of Standards lived. They were within walking and biking distance of their jobs. Many of them were physicists doing research in the area of sound, so perhaps it is not unusual that there was a chamber-music group that played together regularly. The NBS tried to retain its young scientists by offering them free coursework toward their doctorates and by organizing many family activities on the spacious campus. (NIST.)

Hundreds of employees of the NBS assembled for this panoramic photograph on the grounds of the campus in November 1920. It was by far the largest employer in the neighborhood for many

PERSONNEL, BUREAU OF STANDARDS, WASHIN

decades. The photograph also highlights the fact that the scientific core was supported by a large number of men and women of all ages. (NIST.)

This apple tree, said to be propagated from the original tree whose fruit inspired Isaac Newton's gravitational theory, was planted in the pocket park of the International Center in April 2000 by the National Institute of Standards and Technology, the successor to the National Bureau of Standards, now located in Gaithersburg, Maryland. (NIST.)

During World War II, security was so stringent at the NBS that Van Ness Street was closed beginning in April 1942 for the duration of the war. Traffic was prevented from crossing through the campus on Van Ness Street, and NBS employees, many of whom were Forest Hills residents, were not permitted to discuss—even in bland generalities—their wartime work. (NIST.)

In November 1906, E. S. Shepherd photographed the Carnegie Institution's Geophysical Laboratory, under construction on Randolph (later Upton) Street. A physical chemist, Shepherd and other staff members of the newly formed laboratory were temporarily located at the U.S. Geological Survey downtown. The staff moved into the "house of dreams untold" in early June 1907. It served in that capacity until 1990. (Geophysical Laboratory, Carnegie Institution Archives.)

The architectural firm of Wood, Dunn, and Deming worked closely with the laboratory's director, geologist Arthur L. Day, in the design of the building. Independent lab units, offices, and a library occupied the ground and second floors, while the heavy high-pressure equipment, machine shop, and power plant were allocated to the basement, where specially designed floors set in sand absorbed vibrations caused by the machinery. Also in the upper floors was space for workers to stay overnight when experiments required 24-hour monitoring. The state-of-the-art science building was cloaked in a popular Spanish Renaissance Revival style that a contemporary architectural critic noted was appropriate to the "climate and the purse of Washington." (Geophysical Laboratory, Carnegie Institution Archives.)

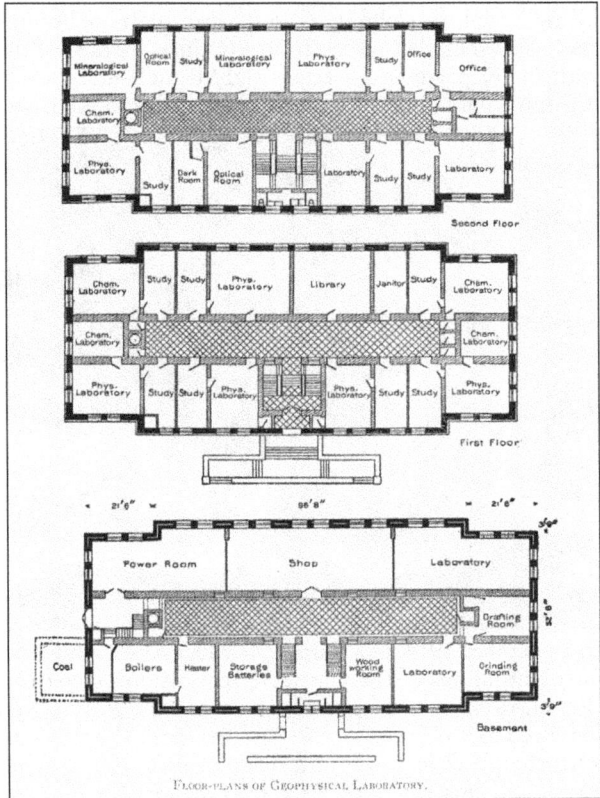

FLOOR-PLANS OF GEOPHYSICAL LABORATORY.

Petrologist N. L. Bowen, right, and O. F. Tuttle work with a cold-seal hydrothermal pressure vessel at the Geophysical Laboratory, c. 1950. The laboratory has conducted considerable research into how high pressure and high temperatures affect the melting and solidification of rocks. During World War I, the laboratory developed high-quality optical glass for the military. War work in the 1940s included research into optimal metals for use in gun barrels, as well as cooperation with the Department of Terrestrial Magnetism in developing proximity fuses for artillery shells. (Geophysical Laboratory, Carnegie Institution Archives.)

In December 1919, Dr. William F. Meggers of the National Bureau of Standards shot this view of the buildings of the Carnegie Institution's Department of Terrestrial Magnetism on Broad Branch Road from a small plane. When the staff moved here in 1914 from its original quarters in rented rooms at the Ontario Apartments, the new building seemed far out in the country, and a streetcar shelter was built for employees at the corner of Thirty-Sixth Street and Connecticut Avenue. (Department of Terrestrial Magnetism, Carnegie Institution Archives.)

In the 1920s, Gregory Breit (right) and Merle Tuve set out to prove the existence of the ionosphere, which they accomplished through the use of the receiver shown here by detecting echoes from pulsed radio waves directed high into the atmosphere. Eventually the Department of Terrestrial Magnetism managed a network of stations monitoring the ionosphere around the world. (LOC.)

Studies involving physics, and especially nuclear physics, became a focus for the department in the 1930s and 1940s. This one-million-volt Van de Graaff generator, being inspected in 1935 by Odd Dahl on the ladder and Merle Tuve below, was developed by the department for use in early atomic physics research. (Department of Terrestrial Magnetism, Carnegie Institution Archives.)

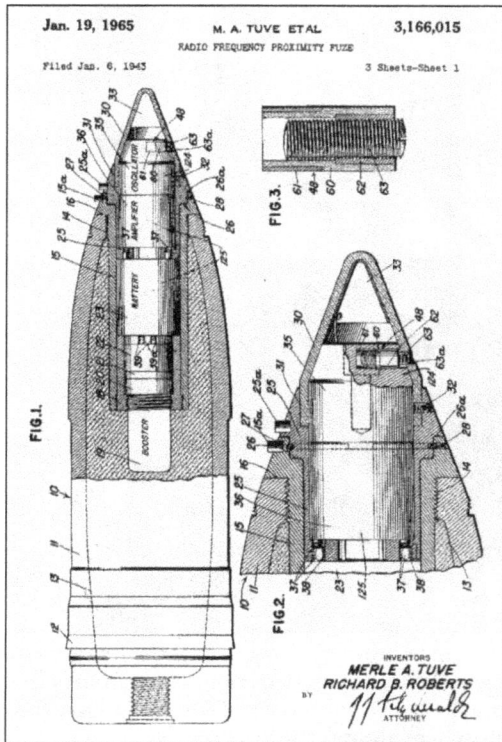

Jan. 19, 1965 M. A. TUVE ET AL 3,166,015

RADIO FREQUENCY PROXIMITY FUZE

Filed Jan. 6, 1943 3 Sheets-Sheet 1

FIG.1.

FIG.2.

FIG.3.

INVENTORS

MERLE A. TUVE

RICHARD B. ROBERTS

BY

ATTORNEY

With the coming of World War II, many of the scientists at the two Carnegie locations voluntarily joined a variety of research projects to assist the war effort. The Department of Terrestrial Magnetism took the lead in developing proximity fuses, in which a small device installed in the nose of an artillery shell used radio frequencies to detect the proximity of the target, causing the shell to explode. These fuses proved especially useful against aircraft at sea, but were also used effectively against the German V-1 bombs aimed at London in 1944 and in ground artillery from the Battle of the Bulge through the end of the war. (Department of Terrestrial Magnetism, Carnegie Institution Archives.)

The International Telecommunications Satellite Organization (Intelsat) Headquarters on Connecticut Avenue is regarded as a fine example of contemporary architecture with its unusual configuration of "pods" and its energy efficiency through the strategic location of glass and sunscreens. The building, completed in 1985, is set on 12 acres and overcomes the great size of its structure in a series of different shapes and angles. The architect of the building is John Andrews. (Photograph by Paul K. Williams.)

Six

SCHOOLS, CHURCHES, AND CULTURAL INSTITUTIONS

BY MARGERY ELFIN

Beginning in 1907, when the Carnegie Institution opened its building on the Upton Street hill, the surrounding block has grown to be an educational enclave. That same year, the Army and Navy Preparatory School opened its doors in houses in the 4100 block of Connecticut Avenue. It was later replaced by the Devitt School in 1924. Sharing space on the hill was the Dumbarton School and College, founded in 1935. As years passed, the Carnegie Institution sold its building to the Levine School of Music, Dumbarton was sold to Howard University, and in 1973, the Burke School occupied some of the buildings that had been prep schools years before. It was founded in 1968 and has been at 2955 Upton Street since 1973. It has expanded into other buildings and is building a new structure to accommodate its student body.

The Sheridan School, at 4400 Thirty-Sixth Street, was established in 1927 near Sheridan Circle on Embassy Row. It was known as Miss Tomlin's School until 1952, when its name changed to the Sheridan School. It has been in Forest Hills since 1966. Solon J. Candage, who began as headmaster in 1967, was instrumental in acquiring a 130-acre wilderness tract near Luray, Virginia, in 1971. Known as the Sheridan Mountain Campus, this site provides students with opportunities in environmental awareness, hands-on learning, and adventure challenges.

The Ben W. Murch Elementary School opened in 1930. Before its inception, a few Forest Hills congressional wives lobbied for its creation as a neighborhood school. The history of Murch has been documented by Ann Kessler, the author of Chapter Seven and a former Murch parent.

The University of the District of Columbia, at 4200 Connecticut Avenue, is a consolidation of Federal City College (a community college) the District of Columbia Teachers College, and the Washington Technical Institute. This merger took place in 1977 with Lisle Carleton Carter Jr. as first president of the university. It serves a commuter population along with a large component of international students with both day and evening courses. It is open to all D.C. high school graduates.

The Howard University School of Law is located at 2900 Van Ness Street, just a few miles from its main campus. In 1904, the land was bought by a holy order, the Sisters of the Holy Cross of Notre Dame, who established an academy there. It grew from an elementary school to a two- year residential college named Dumbarton, which opened in 1935. It closed its doors in 1973 and was sold to Howard University the following year to house its law school. In 2001, Howard built a handsome new library next to the original building.

Adjacent to the law school of Howard University is a nationally known "community music school," the Levine School of Music. It was founded in 1976 as a nonprofit community school. Since 1997, it has occupied the building that served as the Geophysical Laboratory from the time it was built in 1907. The Levine School offers classes for children and adults as well as a summer camp for youngsters at its main campus in Forest Hills and at locations in Maryland and Virginia. Altogether it serves 3,500 students. Its faculty gives concerts regularly in its upstairs auditorium, as do other artists and students during the year.

The congregation of St. Paul's Lutheran Church has a rich history, as it was first organized in 1843 at Odd Fellows Hall on Pennsylvania Avenue. The church next moved to Eleventh and H Streets NW and opened in 1845. St. Paul's moved uptown to Forest Hills in 1926, when it merged with Epiphany and purchased land from the Chevy Chase Land Company on Connecticut Avenue and Ellicott Street. The designers of the church also designed the National Cathedral (Frohman, Robb, and Little). The design was in the style of an English 14th-century church of coarse brick and faced limestone. Directly across from St. Paul's is a pocket park with benches and a bust of a celebrated American Lutheran, John Peter Muhlenberg, who fought in the Revolutionary War.

Work was started in the 1920s, but when the Depression hit, the building was left unfinished, and the congregation worshipped in the basement space; members jokingly referred to this as "underground worship." The lower level of the church was dedicated in 1931, the upper level in 1958, and the education building in 1969. Today it has about 200 active members and 700 members total, drawn from close-in suburbs and from the neighborhood. It is active in the community with a youth group, a preschool, and a homeless shelter in the building.

Located on Chesapeake Street, the Capital Memorial Seventh Day Adventist Memorial Church has been a neighborhood fixture since December 1963, when it moved from Fifth and F Streets NW. The church congregation dates back to the end of the 19th century. The Chesapeake Street property was purchased from the Diocese of the Roman Catholic Church under Archbishop Patrick O'Boyle in August 1959, and building construction began in 1962.

The sanctuary is deliberately simple in design and seats 755 worshippers. Church activities, aside from the spiritual dimension, emphasize a healthy lifestyle, and its annual food and health fairs attest to that. Its members come mostly from the Maryland suburbs and have an amazing diversity of backgrounds, with more than 40 countries represented in its congregation. The church is a familiar neighborhood landmark and has always made space available for Advisory Neighborhood Commission meetings and other community events. It is the voting place for many Forest Hills residents.

One of the last "grand dames" of American society, Marjorie Merriweather Post, purchased a Forest Hills estate, which she named Hillwood, in 1955. This remarkable heiress and art collector wanted a home that would provide an appropriate setting for her impressive collection of Imperial Russian art and French decorative arts and that could eventually be open to the public.

The house, designed by John M. Deibert, had been built in 1926 on 13 acres overlooking Rock Creek Park. Post oversaw the expansion and reconstruction of the original house along with the design of formal gardens. Although she died at Hillwood in 1973, she had looked to the future by bequeathing her art collection and her home and furnishings to the public. Today the elegant mansion is decorated with luxurious fabrics and woods that evokes the splendor of the gilded age. It is filled with extraordinary paintings, icons, and objets d'art. Of particular interest is her Fabergé collection, which includes two eggs that were gifts to his mother from Russia's last tsar, Nicholas II.

A working greenhouse on the estate still provides fresh flower arrangements in the mansion. Visitors can enjoy the gardens and the views along with several unusual attractions, such as the replica of a Russian dacha, a series of "garden rooms," a pet cemetery complete with sculptures of Post's favorite dogs, and a putting green.

Members of the School Safety Patrol at the Ben W. Murch School are seen here about 1965 holding a meeting with a police official to discuss safety problems that have arisen in the school area. The patrol captain at the table is flanked by his lieutenants, whose job it is to supervise the operation of the patrol. This group is typical of the half million boys and girls who protect their fellow pupils at street crossings in 14,000 communities in the United States. (Courtesy Murch School.)

Children are seen here playing in Murch Elementary School about 1965. The school opened in 1930 and serves the neighborhood with prekindergarten to sixth-grade classes. Murch was built after a small group of neighborhood congressional wives lobbied for its creation as a neighborhood school. (Courtesy Murch School.)

Beginning in 1997, the Levine School of Music has occupied the building that originally served as the Geophysical Laboratory of the Carnegie Institution of Washington, built in 1906–1907. It serves 3,500 students of all ages. (Photograph by Paul K. Williams.)

St. Paul's Lutheran Church, at Thirty-Sixth and Everett Streets, is seen here in December 1958. It was organized in 1843 at Odd Fellows Hall on Pennsylvania Avenue downtown, and two years later moved to a location at Eleventh and H Streets NW. St. Paul's moved to Forest Hills in 1926, when it merged with Epiphany Lutheran Chapel and purchased the land from the Chevy Chase Land Company on which it stands today. The church was designed by the same architectural firm as the National Cathedral (Frohman, Robb, and Little). The design was in the style of an English 14th-century church of coarse brick and faced limestone. Work was started in the 1920s, but was delayed during the Great Depression. The lower level of the church was dedicated in 1931, the upper level in 1958, and the education building in 1969 (Courtesy St. Paul's Church.)

The Academy of the Holy Cross School, shown, was later known as Dumbarton College. The Gothic building at 2900 Van Ness Street was built by the Sisters of the Holy Cross and opened in 1935. The Howard University School of Law purchased the building in 1974. The Howard University School of Law had opened its doors in 1869, and in 1872, the law school graduated the first black woman lawyer, Charlotte E. Ray. (Paul K. Williams Private Collection.)

The house pictured above once stood on a huge expanse of land stretching from Brandywine Street to Rock Creek Park. It was built by Dr. Charles Richardson (1861–1929) around 1896 and completed in 1902. At the time its address was 2901 Grant Road, but it is known today as 2901 Ellicott Terrace. By the 1940s, the land surrounding it had been reduced to 17.5 acres, further reduced in the 1950s as homes were constructed on what was now a cul-de-sac. The home was donated by its owner around 1961 to the Archdiocese of Washington, and became a residence for nuns belonging to a Belgian order, the Order of Perpetual Adoration. A chapel was added to the house in 1964. Today the home belongs to the Oblate Sisters of the Holy Eucharist. They are from Mexico and hold masses every day with visiting priests and neighbors. (Photograph by Barbara D. Bates.)

The future site of the Capital Memorial Seventh-Day Adventist Church at 3120 Chesapeake Street is seen here just prior to its construction in the spring of 1962. Designed by architect Harold E. Wagner, the church had a seating capacity of 755 when it opened in the fall of 1963. The facade went through several design phases before the final selection was determined. Some early renditions showed three large white angel sculptures on the western facade. (Courtesy Seventh-Day Adventist Church.)

In 1955, Marjorie Merriweather Post purchased the estate at 4155 Linnean Avenue, built in 1926, which she named Hillwood. This remarkable heiress and art collector wanted a home that would provide an appropriate setting for her impressive collection of Imperial Russian art and French decorative arts. (Used by permission of Hillwood Museum and Gardens.)

The French Drawing Room at Hillwood is seen here in the 1950s. The lavish 13-acre estate overlooks Rock Creek Park. Post oversaw the expansion and reconstruction of the original house along with the design of formal gardens. Although she died at Hillwood in 1973, she had looked to the future by bequeathing her art collection and her home and furnishings to a foundation that would open the house museum and garden to the public. (Used by permission of Hillwood Museum and Gardens.)

Marjorie Merriweather Post is shown here in May 1969 hosting a gracious garden tea party on the lavish grounds of the Hillwood estate. The house had originally been designed in 1926 in a neo-Georgian style by the architect John M. Deibert for Col. and Mrs. Henry Parsons Erwin. (Used by permission of Hillwood Museum and Gardens.)

Despite her imperious bearing, Post could be very comfortable with ordinary people. She loved square dancing and movies and would often entertain her guests informally with popcorn and a movie in her house. Youngsters from Battle Creek High School in Michigan are shown here in May 1963 in the dining room at Hillwood. (Used by permission of Hillwood Museum and Gardens.)

Post is seen here in her prized Japanese garden in May 1963, showing its intricate features to students from Battle Creek High School in Michigan. (Used by permission of Hillwood Museum and Gardens.)

The Edmund Burke School was founded in 1968 and has been at 2955 Upton Street since 1973. It includes grades 6 through 12. Its location was once the site of other historic preparatory schools: the Army and Navy Preparatory School and the Devitt Preparatory School. It razed a large house at 4101–4105 Connecticut Avenue in 2002 to commence construction of a new facility. (Courtesy Burke School.)

Students hang playfully out the window of a Sheridan school bus in the 1970s. The school is located at 4400 Thirty-Sixth Street and was founded in 1927 as a preschool near Sheridan Circle. It was known as Miss Tomlin's School until 1952, when its name was changed to the Sheridan School. The school has been located in Forest Hills since 1966 and now goes through eighth grade. It's headmaster in 1971, Solon J. Candage, was instrumental in acquiring a 130-acre wilderness tract near Luray, Virginia, in 1971, known as the Sheridan Mountain Campus. (Sheridan School.)

Nearly 22 acres of the former National Bureau of Standards property were designated for the campus of the Washington Technical Institute, which merged with Federal City College and the District of Columbia Teachers College in 1976 to become the University of the District of Columbia. Designed by Charles and Robert Bryant and Ellerbe Becket, Inc., the school's 12 buildings were constructed over a 20-year period beginning in 1976 and were plagued by delays and charges of shoddy construction. In this April 1981 view, the Administration Building is on the left with the as-yet-unoccupied Allied Health Building to the right. In 2006, the university enrolls more than 5,000 full- and part-time students in graduate, undergraduate, and associate degree programs. (MLK.)

Seven

FOREST HILLS
CITIZENS ASSOCIATION
By Ann Kessler

The Forest Hills Citizens Association was organized in 1929 by area residents with a common desire to keep their newly created neighborhood beautiful and unspoiled. A meeting to elect officers was held on May 9, 1929, at the Methodist Home on Connecticut Avenue, at which George Esch was elected the first president. The name was chosen over the proposed Azadia Citizens' Association (after the Shoemaker estate), as it represented a new, modern name for the area. The founders were mostly retired men from the military or scientific circles. The sole woman organizer was Leslie Boudinot Flenner Wright, an attorney and civic activist, who was married to a chemist with the Food and Drug Administration. She became the first secretary of the association in 1929 and served as president from 1938 to 1941 and from 1956 to 1958. She was one of the driving forces behind the association for its first 30 years.

The first directory of the association was published in 1929 with 101 members, most of whom were affiliated with the National Bureau of Standards; Mrs. William F. Meggers, wife of one of the most well-known scientists at the NBS, was a charter member. These first members targeted street improvements as a major goal, working to get Albemarle Street paved and a stoplight installed at Albemarle Street and Connecticut Avenue.

During its early years, the association worked to build the local public schools: Murch Elementary (1930), Alice Deal Junior High School (1931), and Woodrow Wilson Senior High (1935). In this effort, Mrs. Wright was aided by Mrs. Burton K. Wheeler and Mrs. Gerald P. Nye, wives of two United States senators who lived in Forest Hills. By 1935, the association was involved in various citywide issues (such as the federal government's responsibility to make a payment to the District government to partially cover its expenses) and local issues (such as the restitution of streetcar service on Connecticut Avenue between Calvert Street and Chevy Chase Circle).

The association worked for years on the creation of a neighborhood playground. In 1942, land for a neighborhood park was finally obtained through the Congressional Capper-Crampton Act for preserving open areas in residential neighborhoods. Through this act, 3.27 acres in Forest Hills was assigned it to the District government, and Mrs. Wright appealed to the city to build a playground. The first Forest Hills playground was built in 1956. It has been upgraded and remodeling several times, including the 1982 variation when Mayor Marion Barry planted ivy and again in 1990 and 2000.

The organization played an active role in the development of Connecticut Avenue, advocating smart growth. As Wright said in 1939, "we are just embattled home-owners, forever fighting the encroachments of commercialism." After the Chevy Chase Ice Palace opened in November 1938, the association fought to maintain the family atmosphere built around its ice-skating rink and bowling alley. In the early 1940s, it opposed the addition of boxing matches, a dance hall, and a shooting gallery but supported soldiers on leave using the rink as a place to relax and socialize.

One of the major fights the association waged in protecting the residential character of the neighborhood was the fight over the WMAL tower in 1969 and 1970. The Evening Star Broadcasting Company, at that time the parent of WMAL-TV (now WJLA-TV), proposed constructing a 1,000-foot-tall transmission tower at the corner of Connecticut Avenue and Albemarle Street. While zoning at that time permitted the tower, WMAL needed an exemption to the 60-foot height limit. An attorney was hired, and the organization won this fight and again protected the neighborhood against the "encroachments of commercialism."

The association first learned of the possibility of a rapid transit station in 1963, and for over a decade it advised and negotiated with transit authorities to bring the subway to the neighborhood in a way that would not interfere with its quality of life. While supporting the building of a subway station (originally to be called Forest Hills), the association was concerned about traffic control, parking facilities, and the construction of mixed-use buildings. By the time the Van Ness Metro station opened in December 1981, the association warmly welcomed Metro to the neighborhood.

In the 1960s, the association worked with the Washington Technical Institute (WTI) and the State Department to plan the development of the former NBS property. The association advocated on-site parking, landscape screening, effective traffic management, and a residential parking sticker program. In 1968, WTI opened at Van Ness with 1,000 students. Eventually WTI would expand its campus and become part of the University of the District of Columbia.

The association has also regularly sponsored social events for residents of the area, providing opportunities for neighbors to meet neighbors. These occasions have included spring social meetings held at area embassies such as Netherlands, Kuwait, Peru, Ghana, Jordan, and Austria and at cultural institutions like Hillwood. Other events for the whole family took place at Peirce Mill and the Forest Hills playground. Picnics and Halloween parades were part of the family fun organized by the association for years.

George Esch was elected the first president of the newly created Forest Hills Citizens Association in May 1929. George Esch was an examiner for the Interstate Commerce Commission. The first officers of the association also included Mrs. Leslie Boudinot Flenner Wright, one of the few women attorneys in Washington; Edward C. Potter, a retired metallurgical engineer who had been vice president in charge of operations for the Illinois Steel Company; and Gen. Mason Patrick, a retired major general of the U.S. Army and former chief of the Air Corps. (FHCA.)

NEW CITIZENS' BODY ELECTS OFFICERS

George Esch President of Forest Hills Association in Northwest.

A new organization known as the Forest Hills Citizens' Association was formed last night at a meeting of residents of the community in the Methodist Home, Connecticut avenue and Ellicott street. Officers were elected as follows: George Esch, president; Edward C. Potter, vice president; Gen. Mason M. Patrick, treasurer, and Mrs. Charles D. Wright, secretary.

Delegates to the Federation of Citizens' Associations: Col. William R. Davis and Col. Arthur O'Brien.

Members of executive committee: George W. White, Herbert S. Wood, Jesse P. Crawford and James M. Proctor.

The territory of the new association

Heads Citizens

GEORGE ESCH.

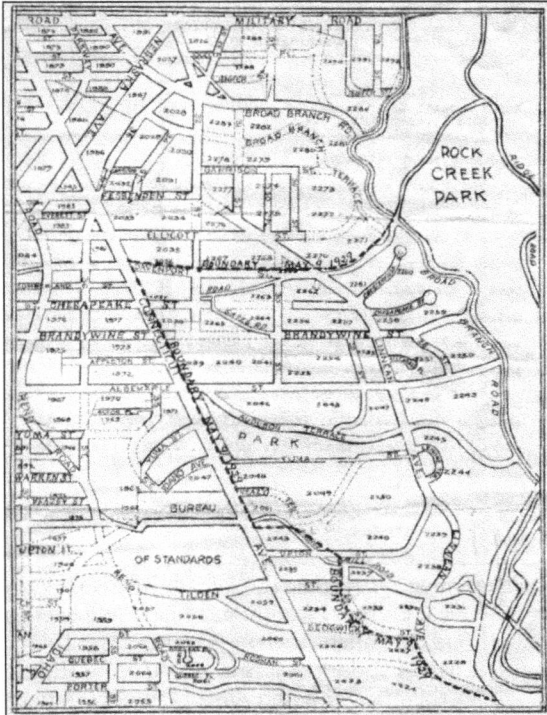

Forest Hills Association Territory is Shown by the Heavy Dotted Lines.

This 1929 map of the Forest Hills Citizens Association territory shows that the founders initially decided that the boundaries of the new association should be Davenport Street on the north, Connecticut Avenue on the west, Van Ness Street to Peirce Mill Road to Twenty-Ninth Street and Linnean Avenue on the south, and Rock Creek Park on the east. An amendment to the association's constitution in 1932 added some territory west of Connecticut Avenue that was bounded on the north by Ellicott Street, the west by Thirty-Eighth Street, and the south by Albemarle Street. (FHCA.)

Forest Hills Citizens Fight
Coney Island Atmosphere

FOREST HILLS Citizens Association serves this general area. President of the association is Mrs. Leslie B. Wright

OCT 20 1940 (inset) POST

This is the twenty-first article in a series about citizens associations in the District and their efforts to make the community a better place in which to live.

Forest Hills Citizens Association, one of the six in the District which are headed by women, celebrates its eleventh anniversary this fall by intensifying its drive to keep Chevy

four terms, and L. A. Carruthers, who has lived on Thirtieth Street since 1914.

Among measures that have been sponsored by the organization, Mrs. Wright lists the naming of the Wood-

One of the few citizens associations in the District of Columbia to be headed by a woman, the Forest Hills Citizens Association was given credit in an October 20, 1940, edition of the *Washington Post* for keeping the neighborhood "a beautiful and noncommercial area." Mrs. Leslie Wright states the association was founded "to combat the neglect which was turning Connecticut Avenue into a Coney Island thoroughfare." (FHCA.)

Soon after the Japanese attack on Pearl Harbor on December 7, 1941, and the subsequent declaration of war, the Forest Hills Citizens Association declared war on tens of millions of Japanese beetles that were devastating the gardens of the neighborhood. Members of the association went door to door to collect funds, and the records show that Mrs. Lyndon B. Johnson and Mr. J. Edgar Hoover donated $4.50 each toward the effort—about the price of a hefty meal on Connecticut Avenue at the time. (FHCA.)

Officers of the Forest Hills Citizens Association in 1955 included, from left to right, Charles A. Burmeister, president; Arthur H. Hahn, secretary; Mrs. Leslie Boudinot Flenner Wright, delegate to the Northwest Council; and Joseph Sanders, chairman of the Zoning Committee. Sanders was chairman of that committee every year from 1929 into the late 1950s. He actively fought for the association against any intrusion in the neighborhood that would damage the quality of life. He was an executive vice president of the Bank of Commerce and president and director of Sanders Investment Corporation, and he had been president of other real-estate corporations. He also had assisted his uncle, Emile Berliner, in the invention of the disc-type phonograph record to play on Berliner's earlier invention, the gramophone. When he died in 1960, he left half a million dollars to be contributed to charities he had supported in his lifetime. (FHCA.)

LS LEADERS—Members of the Forest Hills Citizens' Association meeting. Left to right: Rolland G. Lamensdorf, treasurer; rmeister, president; Arthur H. Hahn, secretary; Mrs. Leslie B ate to the Northwest Council, and Joseph Sanders, chairman o ommittee.—Sta. Staff Photo.

Hills Unit Builds
on of Alertness

Sweeping Probe
Of School System
In D. C. Urged

On July 4, 1982, the official dedication of the new Forest Hills playground was held, with Mayor Marion Barry and City Councilwoman Polly Shackleton seen here planting ivy in the Forest Hills playground that day. It was an all-afternoon family picnic with receipts from the food and white-elephant tables going for additional landscaping for the park. (Photograph copyright Beverly Rezneck.)

At the first of a series of July Fourth picnics held at the Forest Hills Playground beginning in 1985, City Council Chairman David Clarke is seen at left discussing the event with Stephen "Pat" Belcher, treasurer of the association from 1981 to 1996, and Shari Barton, president from 1969 to 1971 and 1985 to 1987. Activities included a tennis tournament, games for children, refreshments, a raffle, entertainment, and fireworks. Families would come, eat, and greet neighbors, sing a few patriotic songs, and then stay for a short fireworks program at dusk. (FHCA.)

Halloween has been an occasion for an association-sponsored family event since 1932, when H. C. Dickinson created a haunted house on wheels for the Halloween parade. The association contributed annually to the D.C. Recreation Department/Chevy Chase Community Center's Halloween party from the 1940s through the 1970s. In 1985, under the leadership of Pres. Linda Swanson, the association began the tradition of holding its own neighborhood parade, complete with band, seen here. (Photograph copyright Beverly Rezneck.)

Eight

FAMOUS AND INFAMOUS
BY REBECCA A. T. STEVENS
AND JUDITH L. SHULMAN

As you walk, bike, or drive through Forest Hills, did you ever wonder who lives in all those houses today and who has lived in them in the past? This chapter takes a brief look at some of the famous and occasionally infamous people who in the past have called Forest Hills their home.

This neighborhood has been populated by a heterogeneous group of residents, diverse ethnically, financially, and professionally. But unlike most of America, our neighborhood is in Washington, D.C. Those who lived here were attracted to the city because it is our nation's capital. The people who called Forest Hills home were civil servants in all three branches of government, including two presidents and at least one Supreme Court justice, as well as the journalists who reported on them, the international community who interacted with them, the intellectuals who advised them, and the local business owners who enabled Forest Hills residents to live, work, and play in this city.

The first residents of the neighborhood, as pointed out in Chapter One, were American Indians who used the natural resources—water, wildlife, and plants for food and shelter, as well as the flint stones found in abundance to make tools. The next wave of residents were farmers who plowed the soil, planted crops, and set up a series of gristmills along Rock Creek, the eastern border of the neighborhood. These residents were undoubtedly famous in their own time, but their accomplishments are now largely forgotten, lost to all but a few historians.

Perhaps the first famous early resident was James Wormley (1819–1884). He was born a free African American in the District of Columbia and owned a farm that included the land now occupied by the University of the District of Columbia at the corner of Van Ness Street and Reno Road. Wormley was a successful businessman who owned the Wormley Hotel at Fifteenth and H Streets NW, which served the rich and powerful of Washington from 1871 until his death in 1884. He was also instrumental in establishing free public education for African American children in the city.

Other locally and internationally important business people also lived in Forest Hills. Hugo Worch (1855–1938) owned and operated a music business at 1110 G Street NW in downtown

Washington. He served as Honorary Custodian of Musical Instruments at the Smithsonian from 1921 to 1936 and resided in a large stone house at 3000 Albemarle Street.

In the same year that Worch died, another neighborhood resident, N. M. "Izzy" Cohen (d. 1995), cofounder of Giant Food, Inc., opened his first store. This store was the beginning of what was to become the dominant supermarket chain in Washington and the surrounding areas for decades. The stores remained a family-operated business until sold in 1998 to Ahold, an international company. Cohen lived at 2925 Albemarle Street, a house that is still in the family.

Probably because of its easy access to downtown and its pleasant, green, leafy setting, Forest Hills became home to many national and local business leaders. Marjorie Merriweather Post (1887–1973), owner of Postum Cereal Company, one of the nation's first important women corporate executives, bought and renovated a house at 4155 Linnean Avenue. In addition to her corporate work, Post was an art collector and philanthropist. Today her home is known as the Hillwood Museum, which she founded to share her extraordinary collections and gardens with visitors.

Fred S. Kogod (1900–1956) lived at 2916 Albemarle Street. He was a multifaceted businessman who cofounded the local KB Cinema Chain with his cousin Max Burka, also a Forest Hills resident. Another of Kogod's businesses first air-conditioned the White House and the Supreme Court building. Kogod also served as a District of Columbia commissioner in the days before home rule.

Other notable business leaders were David Lloyd Kreeger (1909–1990), Morris Gewirz (1898–1973), and Albert Small Sr. (1902–1987). Kreeger, who lived at 3201 Fessenden Street, was the president and owner of the Government Employee's Insurance Companies (GEICO) and was designated Washingtonian of the Year in 1974 by the *Washingtonian Magazine*. Both Gewirz, who lived at 3101 Davenport Street, and Small, who lived at 3245 Ellicott Street, were real-estate developers, building offices and residences for the growing metropolitan area. All three of these men were philanthropists whose legacies to museums and social action organizations continue to benefit the Washington community and the nation.

Philanthropist Isabel Valley January Brookings (1876–1965) also resided in Forest Hills at 2700 Upton Street. She helped found the Brookings Institution, one of this country's foremost "think tanks," providing research and advice to public and private leaders for over 60 years. Another resident who played an important role in advising our national leaders was David Hunter Miller (1875–1961). Miller, who lived at 2610 Tilden Place, was the legal advisor to the American Commission for the Paris Peace Conference (1917–1919) and helped draft the League of Nations Charter.

One of Miller's neighbors, Milton Harris (1908–1991), was a noted scientist and philanthropist who encouraged scientific research, establishing the first fully endowed chair in the Department of Chemistry at his alma mater, Oregon State University. He was a chemist for the Bureau of Standards and went on to become a director and vice president of the Gillette Company. Harris invented waterproof, flameproof, and rot-proof textiles, and was the holder 35 patents. Harris lived in a house at 4101 Linnean Avenue, which has since been replaced by a larger home.

Milton Harris's next-door neighbor at 2605 Tilden Place was Martin Agronsky (1915–1999), one of the most prominent journalists who have lived in Forest Hills. Agronsky was a war correspondent, print and television journalist, and host of "Agronsky and Company," one of the first journalist-as-talking heads television shows, which set the standard for this genre. Agronsky was joined in the neighborhood at 3116 Fessenden Street by Carl Rowan (1925–2000), a pioneering African American journalist and statesman. Rowan was a print and television journalist, a deputy secretary of state, United Nations delegate, ambassador to Finland, director of the U.S. Information Service, and founder of Project Excellence, which funds scholarships for African American students.

Gen. Mason M. Patrick (1863–1942), 3010 Albemarle Street, commanded the United States Air Service during World War I. After the war, he was instrumental in changing the name of the service to the Army Air Corps in 1926; the Air Force would emerge as a separate entity in 1947. Brock Adams (1927–2004) lived in 3002 Albemarle Street, the house adjacent to the one owned by Patrick. Adams was a congressman, senator, and secretary of transportation who retired from politics amid allegations of sexual misconduct. Arthur Goldberg (1908–1990) lived farther down Albemarle Street at 2811. He had a long and distinguished career in government, which included serving as secretary of labor, Supreme Court justice, and American ambassador to the United Nations. J. Edgar Hoover (1895–1972) lived at 4936 Thirtieth Place. He served as director of the FBI for 48 years, from 1924 until his death in 1972. Hoover was the dominant figure in shaping the FBI for nearly half a century, but older residents recall him offering rides to the local elementary school from the bus stop in his government limousine when the weather was bad.

Forest Hills has been home to two presidents of the United States, Harry S Truman and Lyndon B. Johnson. Truman lived in an apartment at 4701 Connecticut Avenue while he was vice president, and he continued to live in it for two weeks after he assumed the presidency following Franklin Roosevelt's death. Lyndon Johnson, while a United States senator, lived at 4921 Thirtieth Place, across the street from J. Edgar Hoover.

Forest Hills was and is the home of many nationally and internationally known politicians, journalists, business people, and a host of other professionals who serve the country and the community. Nevertheless, it remains a neighborhood, like any other, whose individuals and families interact on a daily basis in its schools, playgrounds, shops, and across their backyard fences.

James Wormley was painted by well-known society artist Henry Ulke. Wormley was a freeborn black entrepreneur who began a career as a chef and caterer, a business that made some African-American businessmen fortunes as one of the few occupations in which they were allowed to excel. He owned a farm near where the University of the District of Columbia campus is now situated on Connecticut Avenue when he also owned and operated Wormley's Hotel at Fifteenth and H Street NW. (HSW.)

MORE "TOM SAWYER" THAN CITY BOY

The following is derived from the diary of Fred Rhodes Jr., who was born in December 1913 at 3006 Albemarle Street and grew up next door at 3000.

When a young Fred Rhodes Jr. kept his diary during the mid-1920s, he called it "Four Seasons in the Soapstone Valley" because the valley was his backyard and because nature played a big part in his childhood world. His father owned three lots on Albemarle Street that extended all the way back to the Soapstone Creek, a tributary of Rock Creek. In the early 1920s, the family kept a few cows and a pony, some of which would occasionally wander down to Connecticut Avenue and onto the trolley car tracks, holding up the car until someone would be sent down to the Rhodes's house to ask them to please retrieve their animals.

Rhodes's narrative is full of adventures like "hooking" rides on passing ice wagons and celebrating the birth of a newborn calf. The woods and creek served as the local playground for him and his siblings. They attended the little elementary school in Chevy Chase near Chevy Chase Circle. Fred Rhodes lived to be 87, and after a career as a government lawyer, he founded the Prison Ministry with Charles Colson, serving as its first president.

J. Edgar Hoover resided in this handsome house at 4936 Thirtieth Place. Despite his formidable reputation, he is fondly remembered by adults who grew up in Forest Hills as the man who would give them a ride to Murch Elementary School in his limousine when it was raining. Hoover's exotic recreation room, complete with taxidermy animals and erotic artwork, is seen here inside the house on Thirtieth Place. (U.S. Department of Justice, Federal Bureau of Investigation.)

Harry S Truman is seen here with his wife, Bess, inside their apartment at 4701 Connecticut Avenue, now known fondly as the Truman Building. He was often quoted as having said, "If you want a friend in Washington, get a dog," and appropriately, his old apartment building is one of the few that accepts dogs today. (Matt Conley, Truman Library.)

Harry S Truman and his daughter, Margaret, are seen here in their apartment at 4701 Connecticut Avenue playing records for a publicity photograph taken during his senatorial campaign in 1940. After he assumed the presidency following Roosevelt's death, residents of Forest Hills remember lining up in front of the apartment and applauding him as he left each morning for his new job in the White House. (Truman Library.)

Sen. Lyndon B. Johnson (right) was photographed in September 1955, when he lived at 4921 Thirtieth Place, shown below, directly across the street from FBI director J. Edgar Hoover. According to some historians, he was a personal friend of Hoover and praised him for his accomplishments at the FBI even when other government officials had serious reservations. Adm. Hyman Rickover (left) and his wife lived in a ninth-floor apartment at 4801 Connecticut Avenue from the early 1940s through the 1960s. Known as the Father of the nuclear navy, he was born in Makow, Russia (now Poland) on January 27, 1900. He immigrated to the United States and entered the U.S. Naval Academy in 1918. While he lived in Forest Hills during World War II, Rickover served as head of the Electrical Section of the Bureau of Ships. (Right, photograph by Thomas J. O'Halloran, LOC; left, Star Collection, MLK.)

Sen. Lyndon B. Johnson (above right) resided in this handsome house at 4921 Thirtieth Place. (Photograph by Judith Shulman.)

Patrick Air Force Base, south of Cocoa Beach, Florida, was named in August 1950 after Forest Hills resident Gen. Mason M. Patrick, who lived at 3010 Albemarle Street. General Patrick had been chief of the American Expeditionary Forces Air Services in World War I and chief of the Air Service/ U.S. Army Air Corps from October 1921 until his retirement on December 13, 1927. (Portrait by Sidney Dickinson, U.S. Air Force Art Collection.)

Morris Kanfer was born in May 1898 and was determined to live to be 100, which he accomplished. He was a real-estate developer, lawyer, and a former president of the Connecticut Avenue Citizens Association. In Kanfer's last years, he was a resident of Forest Hills, where he owned a large tract of land in the vicinity of Connecticut Avenue and Albemarle Street. In 1951, Kanfer, at the height of the Cold War, proposed that the federal government build underground shelters in case of Soviet attack. Kanfer thought his land, just north of the National Bureau of Standards, would be a good place to evacuate the workers; he wanted to lease it to the federal government and testified before the Senate Public Works Committee. His idea was to build government offices that could also serve as bomb shelters on his seven-acre tract. Kanfer's idea died in committee, and a few months later, in partnership with Charles E. Smith, he received approval from the Board of Zoning to construct an eight-story apartment building with up to 532 dwelling units known as the Albemarle House. He had originally requested an 800-unit building. Kanfer's proposed bomb shelter morphed into an underground garage, four levels down. (Photograph by Paul K. Williams.)

Nine

THE INTERNATIONAL PRESENCE

BY MARGERY ELFIN

As the capital of the United States, Washington is home to more than a hundred embassies. The term *embassy* can refer to both the actual residence of the ambassador and the chancery where business is conducted. In the early years of our country, many foreign governments bought their residences from robber barons, who had made great fortunes and built mansions in Washington where they could live a grand lifestyle and maintain proximity to the seat of power. A good number of these embassies are still concentrated along Massachusetts Avenue on Embassy Row and up Sixteenth Street, which is situated on the axis of the White House. Their size and elaborate style were intended to project importance.

As the number of independent nations increased after World War II, many countries looked for locations outside the downtown perimeter to meet their growing needs for office space. Often, in the case of new nations, it was also necessary to find appropriate ambassadorial residences.

After the National Bureau of Standards vacated its vast property and moved out to the Maryland suburbs, the federal government turned the extensive landholding into an international complex. In 1968, a master plan was drawn up by the renowned architect Edward Durrell Stone that led to Forest Hills becoming home to what would eventually be 19 chanceries in one central location, in addition to several more residences and chanceries throughout the neighborhood. Initially all the embassies to be built in the International Center were required to have their designs approved by the National Capital Planning Commission and by the Washington Fine Arts Commission. The designs were intended to reflect the spirit of the country represented.

Embassies and chanceries in Forest Hills range from Austria to Zaire (now the Democratic Republic of Congo). Some are relatively modest residences compatibly located side by side with other homes. Some, like Peru and Italy, resemble embassies of past eras, situated on large estate properties that look like private parks. Many of the newer embassy headquarters in the international center are the work of talented architects who won design competitions in their native countries. The State Department's administrative building dominates the smaller embassies on the south side of the center; based there, the Uniformed Division of the U.S. Secret Service regularly patrols the neighborhood.

There are some unlikely neighbors in the complex. For instance, Israel is the first embassy at the entrance of a circular drive leading to a group of Muslim chanceries, including those of Jordan, Kuwait, and other Gulf states such as Bahrain. Egypt, Pakistan, and Malaysia are on the opposite side of Van Ness Street along with Austria and Slovakia. Singapore is down the hill toward Connecticut Avenue. As this book was written, China was beginning construction of its huge embassy on the last remaining plot of land. Along with the daily business of diplomacy, there are a variety of other activities at the embassies, from evening concerts and cultural programs to formal receptions.

In the more than 30 years since this complex was established, the neighborhood has been tranquil on its hilltop site. Embassy employees and neighbors have access to a jewel of a park beautifully landscaped with flowers and benches. There is an apple tree dedicated to the memory of Isaac Newton and the experiments that were conducted there when the land was home to physics labs at the National Bureau of Standards.

There are other corners of Forest Hills with a strong diplomatic presence. A cluster of embassies borders Rock Creek Park at Tilden Street, including those of the Czech Republic and Hungary along Spring of Freedom Drive and Shoemaker Street. Farther to the west on Tilden Street, one finds Congo, Indonesia, and, closest to Connecticut Avenue, Kuwait. The contemporary Netherlands embassy is on Linnean Avenue just off Upton Street, while more than a mile away, on the other end of Linnean Avenue, is the Peruvian embassy, nearly hidden from view in its magnificent deer park. Within walking distance is the residence of the ambassador of Paraguay. The unique international presence benefits Forest Hills with good design and cultural diversity.

The Peruvian ambassador's residence, built in 1925, is the work of Horace Whittier Peaslee, an architect well known in Washington for his buildings at Meridian Hill and his landscaping work. He designed this house, located at 3001 Garrison Street, for prominent builder Charles Tompkins, an engineer who built the classical Circuit Court House of the District of Columbia, as well as buildings at Georgetown University. The government of Peru acquired the property in 1944. It is a good example of the early-20th-century period in American architecture, when Colonial American themes became popular. What is most spectacular is the setting, which resembles an English deer park and totals 25 acres—probably the largest green space left in Forest Hills. At the handsome iron gates of the embassy is a reminder of its function during the Civil War, when Union soldiers camped out with cannons at the ready at forts encircling the federal city to protect it from a Confederate invasion. A plaque on one of the stone pillars at the entrance reads, "Battery Terrill." (MLK.)

The Embassy of Italy is one of the most magnificent ambassadorial residences in Forest Hills and is known for its extensive gardens. Architect Russell O. Kluge designed the home in 1927. It overlooks Rock Creek Park at 4400 Broad Branch Road, with another entrance on Albemarle Street. It is a good example of the boom times in Washington, when many wealthy people commissioned elegant homes. Over the years, no matter who was resident, the home was the site of extravagant parties and balls. Although one might think it is called Firenze after the city in Italy, the house was actually named after the mother of Col. Robert Guggenheim. The Guggenheims purchased the 59-room stone mansion on a 22-acre site in 1941. Guggenheim's widow later remarried and sold it to the Italian government in 1976. (LOC.)

The Federation of Malaysia embassy was completed in 2002 and serves as a chancery. It is located in the International Center near the Embassy of Pakistan. The architect, Ikatan Cipta Bena, has combined elements of vernacular Malay architecture and colonial British elements in a large and elaborate building. There is a traditional Malay portico at the entry, which is a typical greeting point in Malay homes. From here, The visitor glimpses from here the palatial reception area. This expansive multi-story balcony area is dominated by an eight-foot-long crystal chandelier that hangs over and complements the geometric patterns of the marble flooring. (Photograph by Max Hirshfeld.)

The ambassador of Malaysia enjoys a spectacular view of Rock Creek Park from his residence at 2701 Albemarle Street. The house was built in 1925 to the designs of architect James E. Cooper and originally fronted on Broad Branch Road, but when the last part of Albemarle Street was paved, the house gained a new address and switched its entrance to that side of the house. Before the new embassy was built, the spacious lawn of the residence provided a verdant setting for Malaysia's National Day Celebration in September. The house originally belonged to Sen. Thomas Vidal of Oklahoma, the grandfather of author Gore Vidal. It was purchased from succeeding owners in 1957 by the newly independent state of Malaya for their first ambassador to the United States. (Photograph by Andrew J. Glass.)

The Austrian embassy opened on October 26, 1991. It was the first embassy constructed on the north side of the International Center. A Washington architect, Leopold Boeckl, designed the post-modernist limestone building. He is the son of the prominent Austrian painter and sculptor Herbert Boeckl. Its most striking feature is an interior atrium, which provides a space for cultural events, yearly commemorations of Mozart's birthday among them. (Photograph by Max Hirshfeld.)

Egypt's embassy recalls the days of the pharaohs with monumental pilasters at the entrance of the building. The design for the building, opposite the Austrian embassy, originated with the Shehata Consulting Bureau in Egypt. (Photograph by Paul K. Williams.)

Israel was the first country to apply for space in the International Center, and its embassy is situated on a corner lot at Van Ness Street and Reno Road. The final design, after considering many alternative proposals, was approved in November 1978 and has a Middle Eastern flavor. The building is of buff-colored brick recalling the yellow stone of Jerusalem with deeply recessed windows crowned by arches. A large brick courtyard provides an entrance behind a gatehouse and a security fence. The interior decor showcases Israeli art and incorporates many Oriental Jewish motifs. (Photograph by Max Hirshfeld.)

The State Department's administrative center on International Drive looms over the foreign chanceries like the imposing watchdog it is. It is much larger than any other building in the complex and combines the Mediterranean theme of its red tile roof with the post-modern Palladian details of the arched windows, along with other large glass elements that resemble a contemporary American office building. (Photograph by Mel Elfin.)

The embassy of the Czech Republic, seen here, shares a beautiful piece of wooded land near Peirce Mill at the edge of Rock Creek Park with the embassy of Hungary and the residence of the Czech ambassador, a grand house built in 1927 to the designs of architect James E. Cooper. The chancery, typical of American architecture of the late 1960s, was built when the Soviet government persuaded Czechoslovakia to move from downtown to a more secluded location. The architect was Walter Peter, a Washingtonian. (Photograph by Paul K. Williams.)

The Hungarian embassy, as in its actual geographic location, is a close neighbor of the Czech Republic in the District of Columbia. Its small-scale building is designed in standard 20th-century contemporary style. On the lawn in front of the building is this sculpture, which honors a Hungarian-American soldier, Michael Kovacs, who fought in the Battle of Charleston in the Revolutionary War. (Photograph by Paul K. Williams.)

The embassy of the State of Kuwait, located on Tilden Street, includes both an ambassadorial residence and the embassy in one structure designed by Van Fossen Schwab. Built in 1964, its graceful arched facade echoes the Moorish style, a theme carried out in the interior decoration of the building. The Fountain Room (left) is used for formal seated dinners. The Blue Room (right) at the Kuwaiti embassy is named for the beautiful blue of the tile fireplace. Over the fireplace are three minaret-shaped carved niches. Rich wood-paneled walls frame the room, and sofas with lots of cushions to make it a comfortable space for conversation. (Embassy of Kuwait.)

Ghana's embassy sits side by side with the embassy of Israel. The architect was Leon Brown, a professor of architecture at Howard University for 25 years and mentor to many young Washington architects who constructed residences in Forest Hills in the 1970s. Although the embassy of Ghana is built of marble and bronze glass, it aims to recreate a more African setting with its interior courtyard and garden designed to resemble a rain forest. (Photograph by Paul K. Williams.)

The solid-looking fieldstone residence built in 1927 at 3101 Albemarle Street was purchased in 1979 by the Polish People's Republic from private owners. It had once been part of one of the earliest tracts of land recorded in Forest Hills, called Azadia. Another of the many substantial homes built in Forest Hills in the late 1920s, it was designed by architect John A. Weber. (Photograph by Paul K. Williams.)

The first ambassador to inhabit the residence an Albemarle Street was Romuald Spasowski. When the communists imposed martial law on Poland in December 1981, Spasowski applied for political asylum in the United States. President Reagan granted him asylum; the Warsaw government promptly sentenced him to death and took his citizenship and property. He was the highest-ranking communist official ever to defect to the West and said in numerous speaking engagements that he wanted to show support for Lech Walesa and the Solidarity movement. The house remained vacant for some time while Ambassador Spasowski stayed in the Washington area in a "safe house" in Virginia provided by the FBI and later lived in a small apartment in Washington. An ardent anti-Communist to the end of his life, Spasowski penned an autobiography titled *The Liberation of One* in 1987 and died in 1995 in Oakton, Virginia, as an American citizen. (Photograph by Paul K. Williams.)

Situated on Linnean Avenue adjacent to the Hillwood estate is the embassy of the Netherlands. It is a contemporary building with clean, straightforward lines that serves as a good example of the Dutch no-nonsense approach to work and life in general. The design is by Pieter H. Tauber, a Dutch architect who took neighborhood concerns into consideration so that the chancery, though large, does not overwhelm a quiet residential area. (Embassy of the Netherlands.)

Two corners of Albemarle Street are home to ambassadors. The Senegalese flag flies in front of the contemporary home at Albemarle Street and Linnean Avenue (left). The gracious white brick residence at 4501 Twenty-Ninth Street (right) is the home of the ambassador of Malta. It is another example of a moderate-size home bought to serve as an ambassadorial residence, originally built in 1934 to the designs of architect Donald Steele Johnson. (Photographs by Mel Elfin.)

This replica of a Greek statue, a gift to the U.S. State Department from the Greek government, was relocated to the park in the International Complex on September 17, 1965. Her name is *Melpomene*, and she is the muse of tragedy and musical harmony. (Photograph by Mel Elfin.)

This hole in the ground photographed in April 2006 is the beginning of the foundation of the new embassy of China, which is undoubtedly the largest embassy in the international complex. The architectural firm is the Pei Partnership Architects with Chien Chung, I. M. Pei's son, as principal designer. I. M. Pei is best known in Washington for the East Wing addition to the National Gallery of Art. Because of concerns that the 300,000-square-foot building would be incompatible by its size, the design was approved with the caveat that the exterior be softened with landscaping. (Photograph by Paul K. Williams.)

In July 1979, the Nicaraguan embassy on New Hampshire Avenue was seized by revolutionary Sandinistas. They next turned their attention to the residence of the ambassador, Guillermo Sevilla-Sacasa, on Ellicott Street in Forest Hills. Sevilla-Sacasa, with close connections to the ruling Somoza family, was ambassador to the United States from 1936 until 1979. Because he had served so long, Sevilla-Sacasa was dean of the diplomatic corps. When the Sandinistas came to power, he was determined to hang on. He was well known on the party circuit for his old-world manners and his distinguished bearing. These attributes did not serve him well with the Sandinistas, who regarded him as a symbol of class privilege. He was forced to abandon the residence. In the ensuing years, neighbors complained about the condition of the derelict property. In 1981, a fire, strongly suspected to be arson, broke out and destroyed the property. Today several town homes stand where top-level diplomats once partied. Sevilla-Sacasa lived on in Washington until he died at the age of 89 on December 19, 1997. (MLK.)

Ten

AUTHORS
BY DON OBERDORFER

ARTISTS
BY JOAN DANZIGER

FOREST HILLS AUTHORS

Reflecting on his boyhood in Forest Hills, Jonathan Safran Foer wrote in May 2005 in the *Washington Post's Book World* that "it might be the ideal place to become a writer. It's urban enough to offer exposure to a relatively wide mix of people and experiences, and suburban enough to be slow, to give one room to think. I don't know of any other place in America that strikes quite that balance of noise and quiet."

He recalled that he and his older brother, Franklin, invented a secret fort at the base of the hill between Reno Road and Thirty-Sixth Street, created a miniature football field out of a nearby alley, and haunted Higger's Drug Store even without money to buy anything. Increasingly devoted to books after finding a treasure trove of them on the shelves of his parents' attic, Jonathan unsuccessfully applied for a job at Politics and Prose. Authorized by his parents to use a credit card to purchase books, he was a boon to the store. He bought close to $750 worth there after his freshman year at Georgetown Day.

Jonathan Safran Foer went on to become a renowned author (*Everything Is Illuminated*; *Extremely Loud and Incredibly Close*) after graduating from Princeton. His brother Frank (*How Soccer Explains the World*) became a well-known author, magazine writer, and editor of the *New Republic* after graduating from Columbia. Their younger brother, Josh, has written for *Slate*, the *Washingtonian*, and other publications after his recent graduation from Yale. Their father, Albert (Bert) Foer, who still lives in Forest Hills, was asked for an explanation and said at last, "They grew up with words."

Twenty residents appeared on an incomplete list of published authors living in Forest Hills compiled for Forest Hills History Day in October 2004. People who stopped by the authors' exhibit added nine more, and more have since been added. Having at least 33 published authors living in a few blocks appears to validate Jonathan Safran Foer's notion that the neighborhood might be "the ideal place" to write. In addition to authors, Forest Hills is home to a large number of journalists, scholars, lawyers, and other wielders of language, some of whom are very well known for their work.

Bernard Fall (1926–1967), a professor at Howard University, was one of this country's leading authorities on Vietnam. He wrote his epic book, *Hell in a Very Small Place*, at his Forest Hills home, where his widow, Dorothy, still lives and recently wrote his biography, *Bernard Fall: Memories of a Soldier-Scholar.*

Daniel Yergin, an energy expert and chairman of Cambridge Energy Research Associates, won the Pulitzer Prize for Non-Fiction in 1992 for *The Prize: The Epic Quest for Oil, Money and Power*, a number-one national best seller later adapted into a PBS mini-series seen by more than 20 million viewers. He is married to Angela Stent, a professor at Georgetown University and author of *Russia and Germany Reborn: Unification, the Soviet Collapse and the New Europe.*

Charles W. Bailey II, a veteran Washington correspondent and later editor of the *Minneapolis Tribune*, was coauthor with Fletcher Knebel of *Seven Days in May* (1962), a famous political thriller and best seller based on a military insurrection against presidential orders. The book was made into a stage play and a motion picture starring Burt Lancaster, Kirk Douglas, Frederick March, and Ava Gardner.

Kay Redfield Jamison, a professor of psychiatry at Johns Hopkins University School of Medicine, reached within her own traumatic experience with manic-depressive illness to write four highly praised books, including *Exuberance: The Passion for Life* (2004).

Joan Nathan, who has published nine cookbooks, including the recently acclaimed *The New American Cookbook*, began writing three decades ago when she was foreign-press attaché to Mayor Teddy Kollek of Jerusalem and noticed that cultural and religious barriers were breached and even broken down through food.

The most prolific of the authors resident in Forest Hills is the distinguished historian Walter Laqueur, who has written 17 books in the past 35 years, all non-fiction except for two novels. His most recent is *Dying for Jerusalem: The Past, Present and Future of the Holiest City* (2005).

The works of Forest Hills authors range over an extraordinary variety of disciplines and subject matter, including contemporary affairs, science, history, biography, and fiction. One dictionary was even born here—Mike Feinsilber's *Merriam-Webster's Dictionary of Allusions* (with Elizabeth Webber), in 1999.

In addition to those mentioned above, other published authors currently living in the area include Andrew Beyer, Josephine Carr, Edith Couturier, Elizabeth Craft, E. J. Dionne, Margery Elfin, Allan Gerson, Piero Gleijeses, Pierre Guslain, James Hamilton, Val Holley, Nicholas Lardy, Finlay Lewis, Willee Lewis, Neil Lewis, Michael Maccoby, Don Oberdorfer, Joseph Plocek, Mary Ellen Reese, Esther Sternberg, W. R. Smyser, Robert Tomasko, Abigail Trafford, David Von Drehle, Christy Wise, and Alexandra Zapruder.

Forest Hills Artists

Of the many artists who live in Forest Hills, a good number have studios in their homes or have built studios on their property to take advantage of the densely wooded views. As visual artists, they love the neighborhood for its serene beauty and its location on the edge of Rock Creek Park, where they can take a break from working with a walk or a bike ride. They feel connected and inspired by the environment and enjoy the proximity of the downtown galleries and museums. One of the more prominent deceased artists was Jozef Pielage (1902–2000), who taught painting at Howard University and the Corcoran School of Art and lived at 4712 Thirty-Second Street. Joan Danziger, a sculptor, works in her two-story home studio surrounded by her fanciful creations. Light flows in from a 24-foot wall of windows. She says, "I think I got involved with making tree sculptures because of the view from my studio." Her Arts and Crafts home, which dates from 1903, is a perfect venue for integrating her lifestyle and work. "The moment I saw my house I loved it." It seemed a perfect place for an artist to live with her family and many dogs.

Dorothy Fall, an artist resident in Forest Hills since December 1963, comments that she has often used the milieu of her home and garden as subject matter: "the view from my daughter's bedroom window during my landscape period of the 70s; azaleas in the garden during my large flower painting phase of the 80s." She frequently walks the neighborhood, picking up leaves and pinecones for their shapes and colors, which she may use in her three-dimensional paper sculptures or in her handmade paper-pulp paintings. "My carport sometimes acts as my studio. Through a four by six foot screened frame, I pour paper pulp, water streaming down my driveway." *Flower Bed* is one resulting work.

June Shadoan is an abstract painter working in oils and acrylics. Her attractive studio accommodates her large-scale paintings, and the view into the trees provides her with a sense of quietude that is necessary to her work. She has lived in Forest Hills for 15 years, paradoxically having moved "in" from the suburbs to an environment closer to nature.

When Beverly Rezneck and her husband moved into their house in Forest Hills in November 1972, their basement was decorated in the style of a nightclub. The original owners were restaurateurs who had owned a group of restaurants called The Blue Mirror, and they continued this seductive theme in their residence. Today the nightclub effect has been displaced by a photography studio and workspace. The bar now houses computers and printers, providing the tools for Beverly's commercial and fine-art photography business. She frequently uses interesting Washington locations as background for her work.

Annette Polan moved to Forest Hills in 1995 from Capitol Hill. She wanted to find a home where she could build a studio that would provide enough space for the large-scale work that she envisioned. She liked the diversity and ambience of the neighborhood. The large, light-filled studio where she finds her creativity is heightened by a workspace that seems to be at one with nature. These and many other artists continue to find inspiration within the natural and communal setting of Forest Hills.

Pictured here at a festive family occasion, one of the writing Foers, at home in Forest Hills. From left to right are Josh, Bert, Jonathan, Esther, and Frank. (Courtesy Foer family.)

Shown here are just a few of the notable books by the 33 authors currently living in Forest Hills. (Courtesy Dan Oberdorfer.)

Former U.S. presidents and first ladies, among many other authors, present their works at the Politics and Prose bookstore. Seen here is former president William J. Clinton, on hand to sign his memoir with the staff and his admirers. (Courtesy Politics and Prose bookstore.)

Sculptor Joan Danziger can be seen here in her Forest Hills studio, located behind her house. At right is her sculpture *Lady Melinda*, done in 1977 with mixed media. (Photographs copyright George Shadoan.)

Sculptor Joan Danziger's *Bicycle Rider*, is shown here in mixed media. (Photograph copyright Joan Danziger.)

June Shadoan can be seen here in her large Forest Hills studio. (Photograph copyright George Shadoan.)

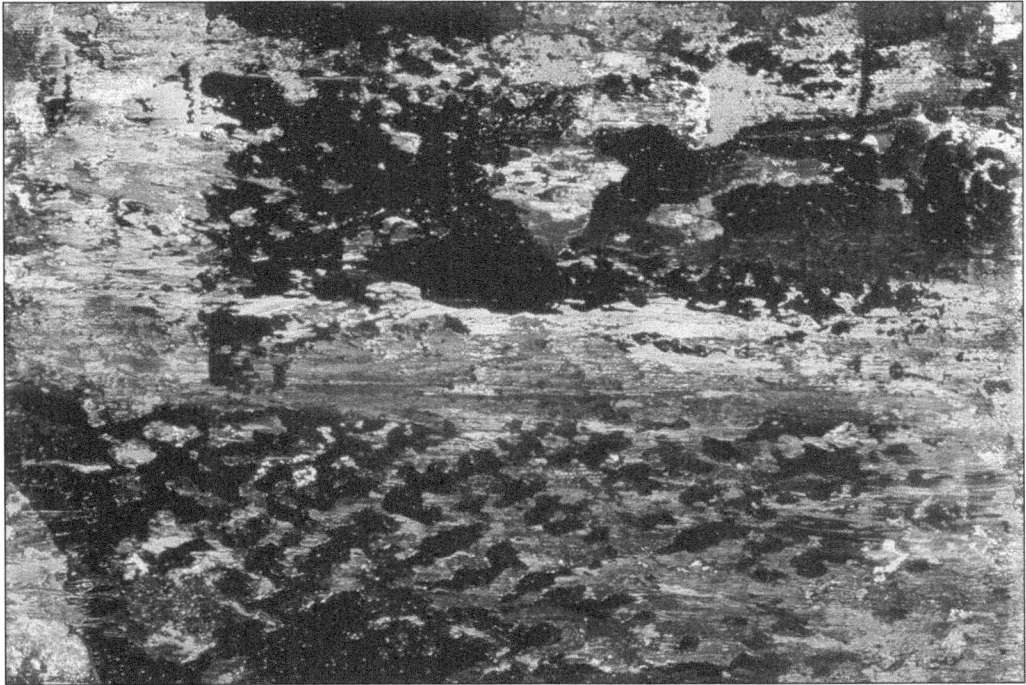

Artist June Shadoan's *Resting in the Sea Gaps* was painted with oil on canvas in 2002. (Photograph copyright George Shadoan.)

Painted in 2002, artist June Shadoan's *A Good Green Grass*, oil on canvas, is pictured. (Photograph copyright George Shadoan.)

Artist Annette Polan's studio looks out into the woods behind her house in the 4700 block of Thirtieth Street and allows her to work on large-scale art pieces. (Photograph copyright George Shadoan.)

Wind and Waves, a performance for installation by artist Annette Polan, was held at the Huntington Museum in Huntington, West Virginia, and featured Mylar balloons, rubber duckies, and mermaids wearing photo-decal bathing suits. (Photograph copyright Annette Polan.)

This large 48-inch-by-60-inch, acrylic-on-canvas portrait of retired Supreme Court Justice Sandra Day O'Connor is by artist Annette Polan. (Photograph copyright Annette Polan.)

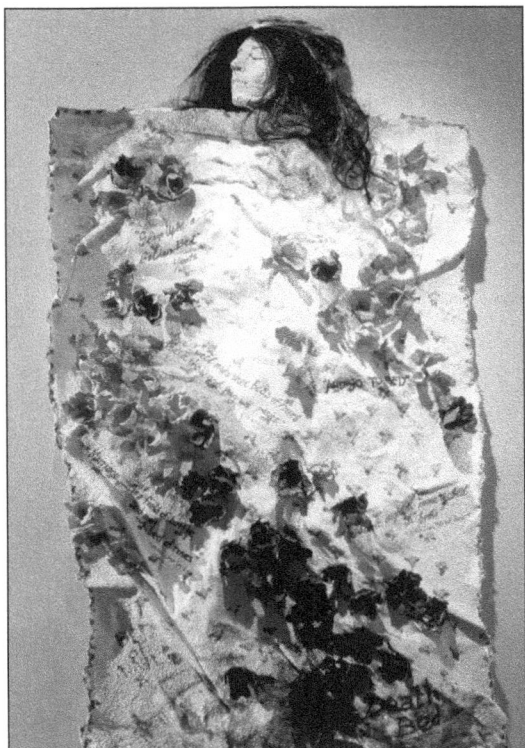

Artist Dorothy Fall's *Flower Bed* is of handmade paper and plaster. Fall stated, "my carport sometimes acts as my studio. Through a four by six foot screened frame, I pour paper pulp, water streaming down my driveway. . . ." *Flower Bed* is one resulting work. (Photograph copyright Dorothy Fall.)

125

Artist Dorothy Fall's *Cambodian Sugar Palms* is a handmade paper pulp painting. (Photograph copyright Dorothy Fall.)

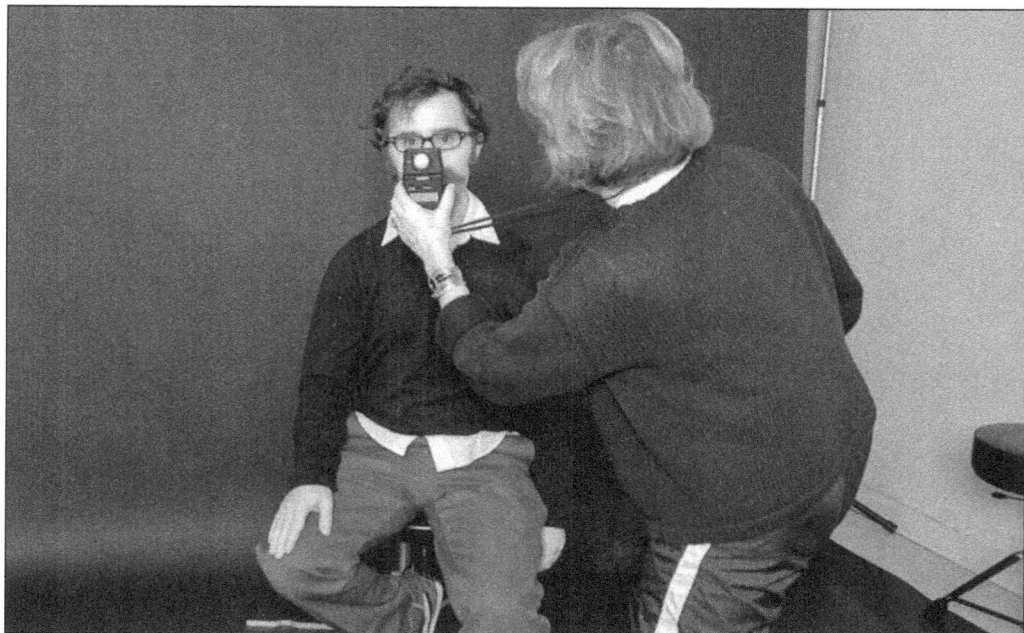

Beverly Rezneck can be seen here using a light meter on a subject in her studio. (Photograph copyright Beverly Rezneck.)

The most celebrated institution in Forest Hills, and in many respects the unofficial community center, is the Politics and Prose bookstore and coffee house at 5015 Connecticut Avenue. Opened in 1984 by Carla Cohen (right) and Barbara Meade, Politics and Prose has grown into much more than a mere commercial establishment. It is a Washington gem that has drawn authors and readers from far and wide and created a special ambiance of its own.

Carla was a novice at the book business—a complex, risky, and highly competitive enterprise. Barbara had previous experience at a bookstore she had started—and then sold—in Potomac. Together they began modestly, first with Carla as owner and Barbara as manager and then as co-owners, as they have been ever since. After only four years, they had outgrown their initial location. On a hot Sunday morning in July, they moved across the street to the current location with the help of friends, relatives, and customers hauling heavy cartons of books. The appreciation and intense loyalty of their neighbors and customers has made the store a very successful business.

Carla's original business plan said, "Politics and Prose will be a bookstore and more. As the name implies, the store will emphasize public affairs and novels. . . . We are hoping to become a gathering place for people who are interested in reading and talking about books. . . . The store will serve as a convener for authors and their readers. . . . We hope to provide greater opportunity for presentation and questions." Since early days, this plan has been fulfilled. Nearly every day, authors come to present their books and meet with readers from the public at the store, which has become a favorite venue for the famous and would-be famous, including many neighborhood and local authors.

In 1993, the coffee house was added, bringing a quiet and convenient place for reading, studying, or chatting, well populated at almost any day and hour. Shortly thereafter, the store took over the space previously occupied by a video store next door, providing additional room for reading groups and eventually a lively children's book section. In 1999, *Publishers Weekly*, the bible of the industry, named Politics and Prose and its owners Bookseller of the Year for the entire country. Through C-Span, which often broadcasts authors' presentations, and through print references and word of mouth, the store has become widely known.

In September 2005, Politics and Prose celebrated its 21st anniversary with panels of local authors of political books, of novels, and of poetry. The store remains the literary heart of Forest Hills and an institution of importance to the community and the wider world.

Visit us at
arcadiapublishing.com

....